FIVE LIVES   FÜNF LEBEN   CINQ VIES

RIEFEN

LENI STAHL

EDITED BY ANGELIKA TASCHEN

TASCHEN

KÖLN LONDON MADRID NEW YORK PARIS TOKYO

© 2000 TASCHEN GmbH
Hohenzollernring 53, 50672 Köln
www.taschen.com

© Leni Riefenstahl
Photos: Leni Riefenstahl Archiv

© for the photograph by Alfred Eisenstaedt:
TimePix/inter Topics
© for the photograph by Lotte Jacobi:
Lotte Jacobi Archives, Diamond Library, University of New Hampshire
© for the photograph by George Rodger:
Magnum/Agentur Focus

EDITOR
Angelika Taschen, Cologne
GRAPHIC DESIGN
Lambert und Lambert, Düsseldorf
APPENDIX TEXT
Ines Walk, Berlin
TEXT EDITOR
Ursula Fethke, Cologne
TRANSLATION
English translation by Steven Lindberg, Pasadena
French translation by Martine Passelaigue, Munich
PRODUCTION
Thomas Grell, Cologne
LITHOGRAPHY AND PRINTING
EBS, Verona
ISBN
3–8228–6025–5 (German edition)
3–8228–6216–9 (English edition)
3–8228–5965–6 (French edition)
Printed in Italy

DANCER
TÄNZERIN
DANSEUSE

ACTRESS
SCHAUSPIELERIN
ACTRICE

DIRECTOR
REGISSEURIN
RÉALISATRICE

PHOTOGRAPHER
FOTOGRAFIN
PHOTOGRAPHE

DIVER
TAUCHERIN
PLONGEUSE SOUS-MARINE

An extraordinary woman with an extraordinary career: This book, *Leni Riefenstahl Five Lives,* reveals in photographs the path taken by a life that spans nearly an entire century. She began as a celebrated dancer in Berlin during the early twenties, became an actress, then finally directed and produced her own films, several of which are among the most influential and most controversial in the history of film. Since the fifties she has traveled frequently to Africa and has lived for extended periods in the Sudan with the primitive Nuba tribes. Though long since a legend, she again attracted worldwide attention with her photographs of the Nuba. Then, at 71, she learned to dive and yet again turned her experiences into art with photographs of the undersea world.

Early in 1998 I visited Leni Riefenstahl for the first time in her house near Lake Starnberg, and we agreed to publish a large illustrated vol-

PREFACE VORWORT PRÉFACE

Eine außergewöhnliche Frau mit einer außergewöhnlichen Karriere: Dieses Buch *Leni Riefenstahl Fünf Leben* zeigt ihren Lebensweg, der fast ein ganzes Jahrhundert umspannt, in Bildern. Sie beginnt als gefeierte Tänzerin im Berlin der frühen zwanziger Jahre, wird Schauspielerin und dreht und produziert schließlich ihre eigenen Filme, von denen einige zu den einflussreichsten und auch umstrittensten der Filmgeschichte zählen. Nach dem Zweiten Weltkrieg reist sie seit den fünfziger Jahren häufig nach Afrika und lebt dort für einige Zeit im Sudan bei den archaischen Nuba-Stämmen. Wieder erregt sie, längst schon zur Legende geworden, weltweit Aufsehen mit ihren Fotos von den Nuba. Dann, mit 71 Jahren, entdeckt und erlernt sie das Tauchen und verarbeitet auch ihr Erleben der Unterwasserwelt wieder künstlerisch in Bildern.

Das erste Mal besuche ich Leni Riefenstahl Anfang 1998 in ihrem Haus in der Nähe des Starnberger Sees, und wir vereinbaren, einen großen

Une carrière exceptionnelle pour une femme exceptionnelle : Le livre *Leni Riefenstahl Cinq Vies* retrace en images presque un siècle de vie. Leni Riefenstahl est d'abord très applaudie comme danseuse dans le Berlin du début des années vingt, elle devient ensuite actrice et, finalement, réalisatrice et productrice de ses propres films, dont certains comptent parmi les plus importants et les plus controversés de l'histoire du cinéma. Après la Deuxième Guerre mondiale, dès les années cinquante, elle se rend plusieurs fois en Afrique et vit quelque temps au Soudan auprès des tribus nouba. Entrée dans la légende depuis longtemps, elle est à nouveau reconnue dans le monde entier pour ses photos de Nouba. À l'âge de 71 ans, elle découvre et apprend la plongée sous-marine, et, une nouvelle fois, elle exprime ce qu'elle ressent à travers des images artistiques.

C'est au début de l'année 1998 que j'ai rendu visite pour la première fois à Leni Riefenstahl, dans sa maison près du lac de Starnberg. Nous

ume on her life. Numerous other visits followed, during which we worked together to select photographs from her extensive, meticulously organized archive, spreading them out on the floor to establish sequences and juxtapositions. While working she would forget her back pain and crawl around on the floor like a young girl, pushing the pictures about to see which ones worked best together. Then she would skip down the steep wooden staircase into her cellar, where her film studio is, to find other, better, and often previously unpublished photographs.

Before we began work, we always had coffee and cake and talked about her life but especially her future projects and travels. I was impressed by her vitality and grace. Her eyes sparkling with curiosity and enthusiasm, her girlish charm, and her seemingly shy smile had me forgetting entirely that she was 97. Although we were more than two

Bildband über ihr Leben zu verlegen. Zahlreiche weitere Besuche folgen, bei denen wir gemeinsam Fotos aus ihrem umfangreichen und präzise geordneten Archiv heraussuchen und diese auf dem Fußboden ausbreiten, um die Abfolge und Gegenüberstellungen festzulegen. Bei der Arbeit vergisst sie ihre starken Rückenschmerzen und krabbelt wie ein junges Mädchen auf allen Vieren über den Boden, um die Bilder herumzuschieben und um zu sehen, welche am besten nebeneinander wirken. Dann springt sie die steile Holztreppe ihres Hauses in den Keller hinunter, wo auch ihr Filmstudio ist, um noch andere, bessere und oft bislang unveröffentlichte Fotos zu holen.

Doch bevor wir mit der Arbeit beginnen, werden immer Kaffee und Kuchen serviert, und wir sprechen über ihr Leben, besonders aber über ihre künftigen Projekte und Reisen. Ich bin von ihrer Lebendigkeit und Grazie zutiefst beeindruckt. Und ihre vor Neugier und Enthusiasmus blitzenden Augen, ihr mädchenhafter Charme und ihr fast schüchtern

nous sommes mises d'accord sur la publication d'un important ouvrage sur sa vie. De nombreuses autres visites ont suivi, au cours desquelles nous avons ensemble retenu des photos parmi ses nombreuses archives, soigneusement classées. Nous les avons étalées à même le sol pour en établir l'agencement général. Elle oubliait en travaillant ses violentes douleurs dans le dos, marchait à quatre pattes comme une gamine, déplaçait les photos pour améliorer l'enchaînement. Puis, empruntant un raide escalier de bois, elle descendait dans sa cave, où se trouve aussi son studio de cinéma, et allait chercher d'autres photos, meilleures encore, souvent inédites.

Mais avant de nous mettre au travail, nous prenions toujours un café et une part de gâteau, parlions de sa vie, de ses prochains projets et voyages surtout. Sa vivacité et sa grâce m'impressionnent profondément. Ses yeux, pétillants d'enthousiasme et de curiosité, son charme juvénile, son sourire presque timide me font complètement oublier que

generations apart, I was never aware of the fact. We worked at such a pace that Leni Riefenstahl's close colleague Ms. Jahn often intervened to slow us down.

Again and again, I tried to imagine this woman working on *Triumph of the Will,* her film of the National Socialist party congress, or on *Olympia.* I see her as an obsessed artist whose only goal was to translate her vision of beauty and aesthetics into film. Even so, her film *Triumph of the Will* was not only a triumph in the history of film, it was also propaganda for a totalitarian regime, a fact that has determined her entire life after the war.

But it is precisely the contradictory aspects of her history that have made her a key figure in the 20th century, just as it is the fact that she is a woman that makes her biography so arresting. In her day she was unique as a woman and as an artist. Only a few women have conquered

wirkendes Lächeln lassen mich völlig vergessen, dass diese Frau 97 Jahre alt ist. Obwohl über zwei Generationen zwischen uns liegen, spüre ich das bei der gemeinsamen Arbeit nie. Wir arbeiten oft in einem so rasanten Tempo, dass Leni Riefenstahls enge Mitarbeiterin, Frau Jahn, des Öfteren bremsend eingreifen muss.

Ich versuche immer wieder, mir diese Frau bei der Arbeit an dem Reichsparteitagsfilm *Triumph des Willens* oder an *Olympia* vorzustellen, und ich sehe sie als eine besessene Künstlerin, die nur ein Ziel vor Augen hat, ihre Vision von Schönheit und Ästhetik filmisch umzusetzen. Doch ihr Film *Triumph des Willens* ist nicht nur ein Triumph in der Geschichte des Films, sondern war auch Propaganda für ein verbrecherisches Regime, was nach dem Krieg ihr ganzes Leben bestimmen wird.

Aber gerade auch das Widersprüchliche ihrer Geschichte macht sie zu einer so herausragenden Persönlichkeit des 20. Jahrhunderts und der

cette femme a 97 ans. Plus de deux générations nous séparent, mais à aucun moment je ne le ressens. Notre rythme de travail est souvent tellement rapide que sa proche collaboratrice, Madame Jahn, doit intervenir pour la freiner.

À plusieurs reprises, j'essaie d'imaginer cette femme réalisant le film sur le congrès du parti, *Le Triomphe de la volonté,* ou bien *Les Dieux du Stade.* Je vois alors une artiste passionnée n'ayant qu'un seul objectif, celui de transposer au cinéma sa vision de la beauté et de l'esthétique. Mais son film *Le Triomphe de la volonté* n'est pas seulement un triomphe dans l'histoire du cinéma, il a aussi servi la propagande d'un régime criminel – ce qui marquera toute la vie de Leni Riefenstahl après la guerre.

C'est précisément l'aspect contradictoire de son histoire qui fait d'elle une remarquable personnalité du XXᵉ siècle ; de surcroît, c'est une femme, et sa biographie en est d'autant plus captivante. Car son rôle est

the male world of directing, and Leni Riefenstahl has influenced the aesthetics of film and photography as few others have done; to this day, many great directors and photographers mention her work.

This illustrated volume shows the astonishing life, the unique career, and the outstanding oeuvre of Leni Riefenstahl. I would like to thank Ms. Riefenstahl for her unusual commitment and enthusiasm in realizing this book. It pleases me that I was able to work with such a special woman and unique artist, and I hope that my own enthusiasm comes across as you read this book.

Angelika Taschen
Cologne, 18 July 2000

Aspekt, dass sie eine Frau ist, ihre Biografie so spannend. In ihrer Zeit ist sie als Frau und Künstlerin einzigartig. Nur wenige Frauen haben die Männerdomäne der Regie erobert, und Leni Riefenstahl hat dabei die Film- und Fotoästhetik wie kaum jemand sonst beeinflusst, viele große Regisseure und Fotografen beziehen sich auf ihr Werk.

Dieser Bildband zeigt das erstaunliche Leben, die einzigartige Karriere und das herausragende Werk von Leni Riefenstahl. Ich danke Frau Riefenstahl für ihr ungewöhnliches Engagement und ihre begeisterte Mitarbeit bei der Realisierung dieses Buches. Ich bin glücklich, dass ich mit einer so besonderen Frau und einzigartigen Künstlerin zusammenarbeiten konnte, und hoffe, dass sich meine Begeisterung beim Betrachten dieses Buches überträgt.

Angelika Taschen
Köln, den 18. Juli 2000

unique pour son époque: rares en effet sont les femmes qui se sont imposées dans l'univers très masculin de la régie cinématographique. Plus que d'autres, Leni Riefenstahl a du reste influencé l'esthétique du cinéma et de la photo; quantité de grands cinéastes et photographes s'inspirent aujourd'hui encore de son œuvre. Ce recueil retrace la vie étonnante, la carrière unique et l'œuvre hors pair de Leni Riefenstahl. Je remercie Madame Riefenstahl pour son formidable engagement et sa très précieuse collaboration dans la réalisation de ce livre. Je suis heureuse d'avoir eu la chance de travailler avec une femme et une artiste aussi exceptionnelle, et j'espère communiquer mon enthousiasme à tous celles et ceux qui ouvriront ces pages.

Angelika Taschen
Cologne, le 18 juillet 2000

DANCER
TÄNZERIN
DANSEUSE

ACTRESS
SCHAUSPIELERIN
ACTRICE

DER HEILIGE BERG 1926

THE HOLY MOUNTAIN   LA MONTAGNE SACRÉE

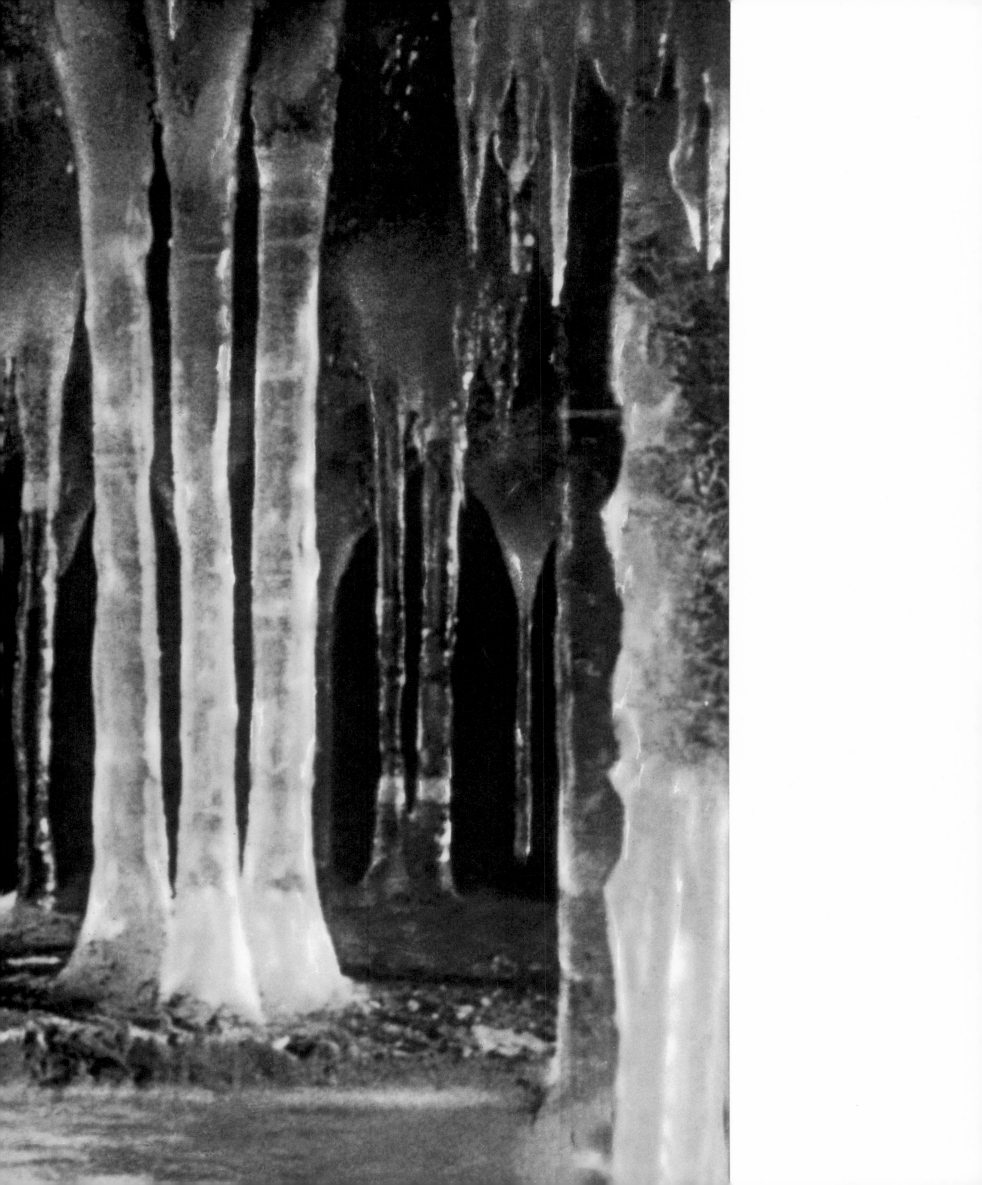

DER GROSSE SPRUNG 1927

THE GREAT LEAP   LE GRAND SAUT

DIE WEISSE HÖLLE VOM PIZ PALÜ 1929

THE WHITE HELL OF PITZ PALU

L'ENFER BLANC DU PIZ PALU

STÜRME ÜBER DEM MONTBLANC 1930

STORM OVER MONT BLANC

TEMPÊTE SUR LE MONT-BLANC

DER WEISSE RAUSCH 1931

THE WHITE FLAME   L'IVRESSE BLANCHE

SOS EISBERG 1933

SOS ICEBERG

DIRECTOR
REGISSEURIN
RÉALISATRICE

1932 **DAS BLAUE LICHT**

1935 **TRIUMPH DES WILLENS**

1938 **OLYMPIA**

1940–1954 **TIEFLAND**

DAS BLAUE LICHT 1932

THE BLUE LIGHT   LA LUMIÈRE BLEUE

TRIUMPH DES WILLENS 1935

TRIUMPH OF THE WILL   LE TRIOMPHE DE LA VOLONTÉ

OLYMPIA 1938

LES DIEUX DU STADE

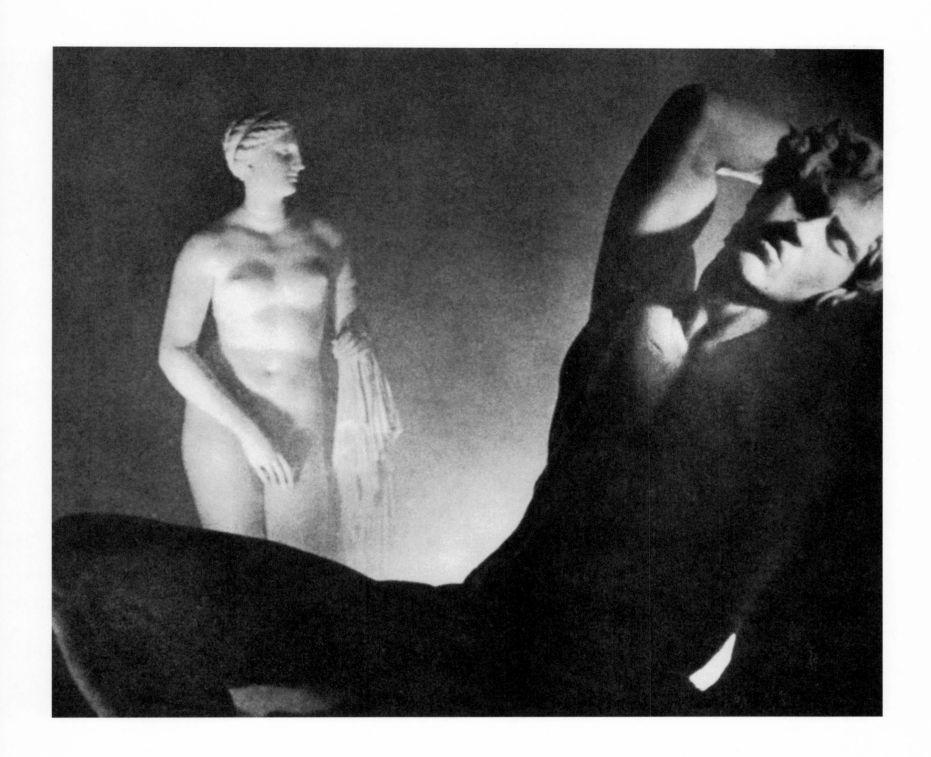

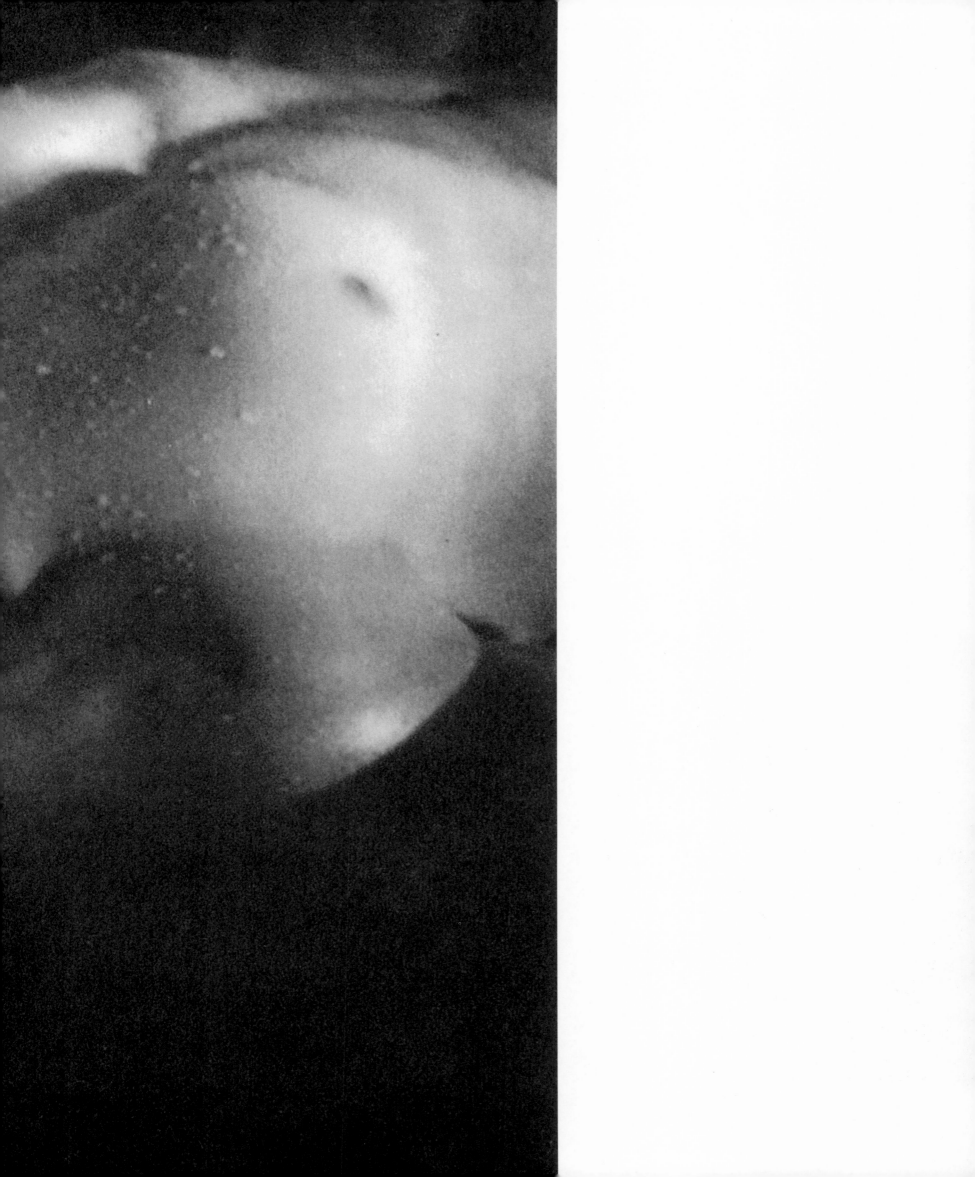

TIEFLAND 1940–1954

PHOTOGRAPHER
FOTOGRAFIN
PHOTOGRAPHE

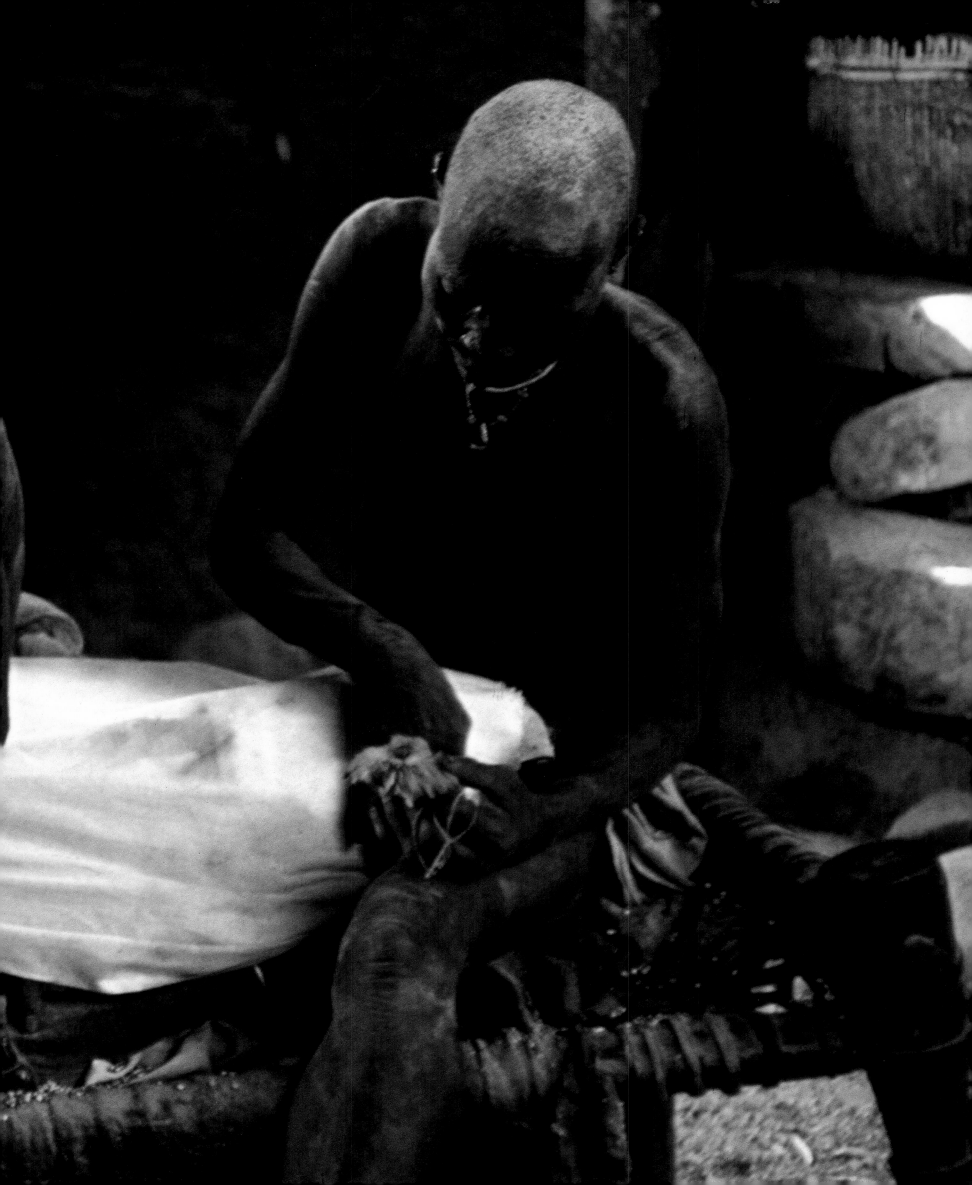

DIVER
TAUCHERIN
PLONGEUSE SOUS-MARINE

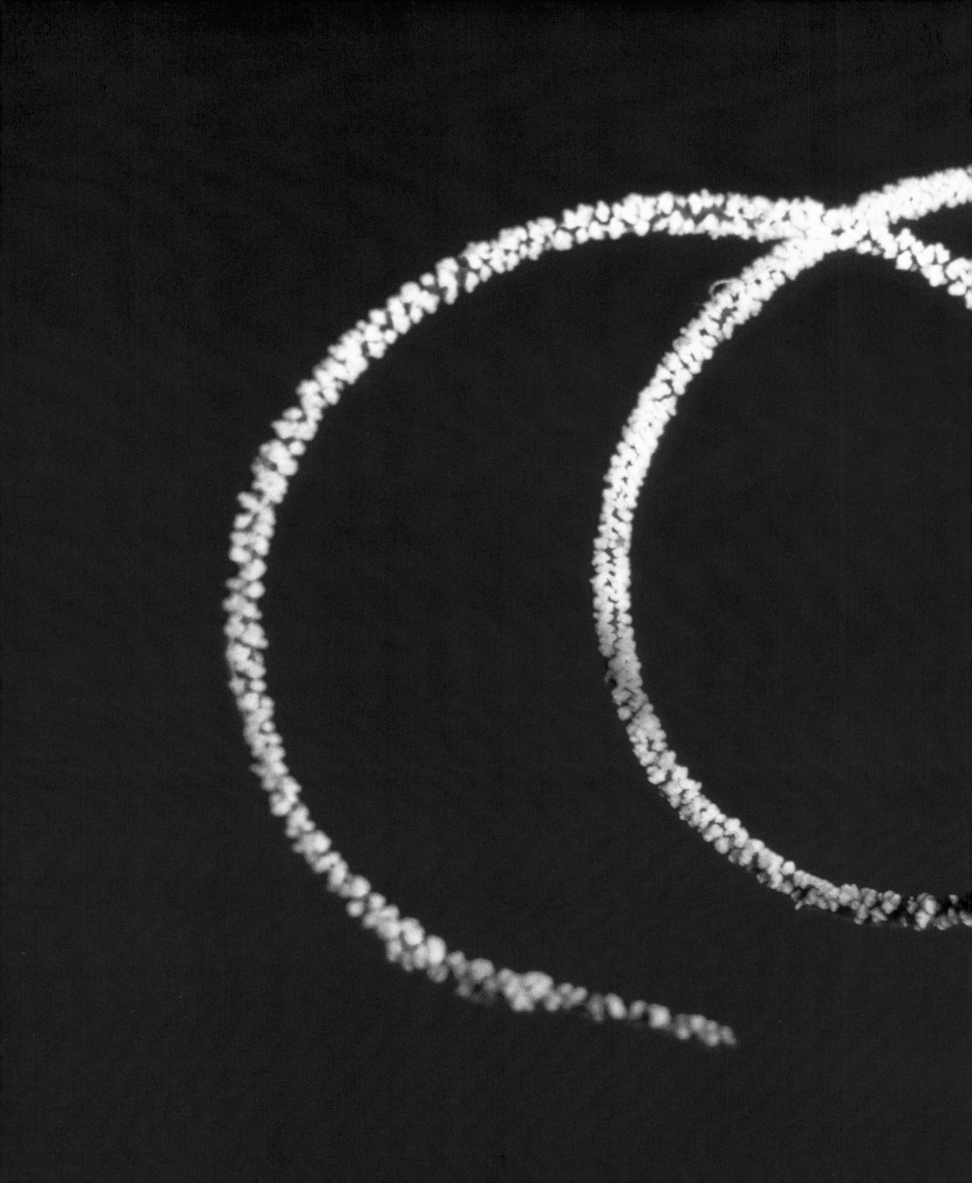

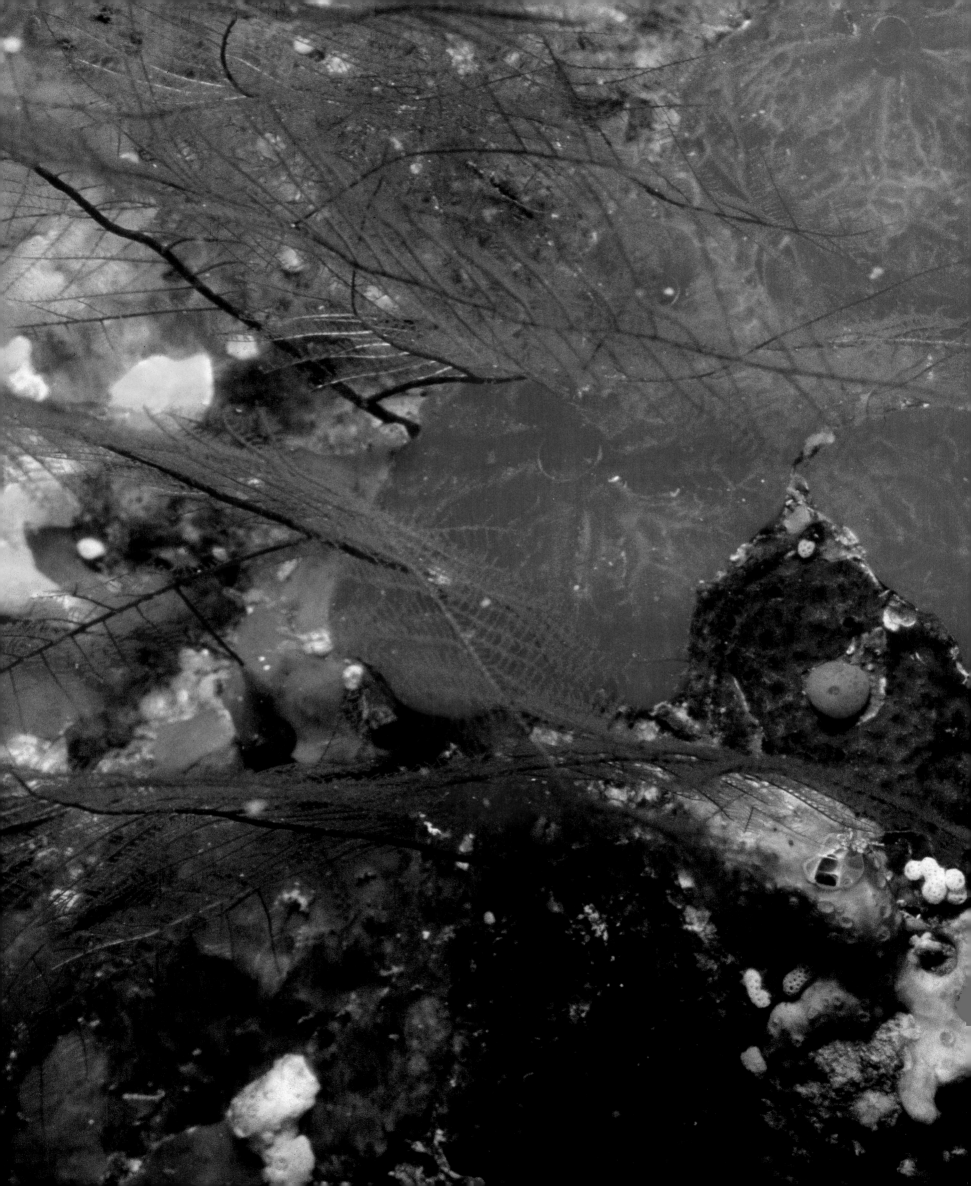

TÄNZERIN DANCER

SCHAUSPIELERIN ACTRESS

THE HOLY MOUNTAIN

DANCER

1 Leni Riefenstahl in her dance *Dream Blossom*, to music by Chopin. This is one of about 15 solo dances that she choreographs herself.

2-4 As a dance student, 1918. At 16, without her father's knowledge, she takes dance lessons at the Helene Grimm-Reiter School on the Kurfürstendamm in Berlin.

5-6 All of these dance photographs are taken around 1923 in the studio of the famous photographer Karl Schenker on Budapester Strasse in Berlin.

7 She choreographs her dance *Valse Caprice* to music that the Italian pianist and composer Ferruccio Busoni dedicated to her.

8-9 In Dresden, enrolled for half a year at the Mary Wigman school, she choreographs *Study after a Gavotte* to music by Gluck and Brahms.

10 In December 1923 Max Reinhardt engages the dancer every night for one week as a solo dancer in his Deutsches Theater in Berlin. It is the only time Reinhardt presents a dancer nightly in his theater.

11-13 Her dance *Arabesque*. In 1923–1924 she completes a tour with more than 70 solo dance evenings in Germany and abroad, in Munich, Frankfurt, Dresden, Zurich and Prague. She is always accompanied by her mother, who sews the dance costumes Leni Riefenstahl designs herself.

14 In the role of Diotima in the film *The Holy Mountain* (1926)

she performs excerpts from her dance cycle *The Three Dances of Eros*. She revises her choreography for this film with an eye to the demands of the new medium.

15 As Diotima in the dance *Surrender*, to music by Chopin.

ACTRESS

16 Publicity still, 1932, for *SOS Iceberg*. Between 1925 and 1933 Leni Riefenstahl plays the leading role in six mountain films directed by Arnold Fanck.

THE HOLY MOUNTAIN
1926

17 UFA publicity still as Diotima. Fanck writes the screenplay for this film for Leni Riefenstahl while she is in the hospital for three months recuperating from a dance injury.

18 In her first film role she plays the dancer Diotima.

19 Luis Trenker as the leading man.

20-21 Filming takes place in the

21   22

THE GREAT LEAP

23   24   25   26

THE WHITE HELL OF PITZ PALU

27   28   29   30   31   32

STORM OVER MONT BLANC

33   34   35   36   37

Grisons, the Engadine Valley, and the Valais Alps.

22 For the final wedding scene Arnold Fanck has a 50-foot-tall stalactite hall of ice constructed on a frozen lake in Lenzerheide in the Grisons.

THE GREAT LEAP
1927

23 UFA publicity still as the goatherd Gita. With her second starring role she decides in favor of a career in acting and gives up dancing for good.

24-25 With Pippa the goat.

26 On the Fensterle Towers in the Dolomites. For her work with Fanck she learns mountain climbing and even barefoot rock climbing.

THE WHITE HELL
OF PITZ PALU
1929

27 Night shot with Leni Riefenstahl and Ernst Petersen. Under the codirection of G. W. Pabst, she turns in her best acting performance under another director.

28 The famous actor Gustav Diessl plays the mountain climber Dr. Johannes Krafft.

29 Publicity still as Maria. With this film Leni Riefenstahl establishes herself as the leading star in mountain films.

30 Climbing on Pitz Palu. The actors film for weeks at temperatures of −18° F.

31 Arnold Fanck tolerates no studio shots or doubles. Here he films the actors as an avalanche descends upon them.

32 Maria and Dr. Krafft wave to the rescue pilot (Ernst Udet).

STORM OVER
MONT BLANC
1930

33 In her fourth leading role, as the astronomer Hella Armstrong, she embodies the modern woman as a scientist.

34 Sepp Rist in his other career, as a police radio operator.

35 Rist in his first role, as the meteorological observer on Mont

Blanc. The amateur actor catches her eye as an excellent skier and he is hired for the film, although the director puts up heavy resistance.

36 This publicity still is taken by Lotte Jacobi.

37-38 During filming the entire crew lives in the Vallot shelter hut on Mont Blanc, at an altitude of 14,000 feet. At night 14 people sleep lying sideways on this wooden platform.

39 The meteorological observer and Hella try out the echo from

38   39   40

41   42

THE WHITE FLAME

43   44   45   46

47

the peak of a cliff near the Grands Mulets on Mont Blanc.

40 Leni Riefenstahl is in the cockpit when the pilot Ernst Udet, in his plane *Motte* (Moth), makes the first landing ever on a glacier, the Mont Blanc glacier.

41 Hella crosses a 150-foot-deep crevasse in the Bosson glacier on a rickety ladder.

42 Rifts in the glacier in the spring. Fanck's films captivate with their stunning shots of the mountain world. Avalanches and

rifts are daily occurrences on the set.

THE WHITE FLAME
1931

43-44 She accepts her first role as a comedienne only in order to finance her own directing project, *The Blue Light*. Here, she plays Leni, a city woman who is spending her winter vacation in the mountains learning to ski.

45-46 Guzzi Lantschner and Walter Riml are both excellent skiers and are often used by

Fanck as actors and stuntmen as well.

47 In the role of Leni from Berlin, she learns to negotiate a small jump.

SOS ICEBERG
1933

48 Publicity still as the pilot Ellen Lawrence, who is searching in Greenland for her lost husband.

49 Sepp Rist plays the leader of the expedition. The whole crew, including two polar bears from

the Hamburg Zoo, is shipped to Greenland in May 1932.

50 Ernst Udet plays a rescue pilot again. Leni Riefenstahl remains friends with him until his suicide in 1941.

51 The film crew lives for many months in a tent camp on the northwest coast of Greenland.

52 The dangerous and arduous filming under Arnold Fanck is described by Leni Riefenstahl in her book *Struggle in Snow and Ice* (1933).

53 The Danish polar explorer and ethnologist Knud Rasmussen, known as the King of the Eskimos, accompanies the crew as an advisor and reports, for example, on the speed of floating icebergs.

54 She is copilot when Ernst Udet crashes his plane *Moth* into an iceberg, as called for in the script. Just before the collision she leaps from the plane into the Arctic water.

55 Ellen and her husband (Gustav Diessl) wait for rescue. This

SOS ICEBERG

48 49 50 51

52 53 54

55 56 57 58

REGISSEURIN DIRECTOR

59

THE BLUE LIGHT

60 61 62

scene is filmed on the Bernina Pass in a reconstructed ice cave.

56 After the plane crash Ellen takes her bearings in the wasteland of ice.

57 Eskimos pass the icebergs in kayaks – a dangerous scene, because the icebergs can break apart unexpectedly at any moment.

58 Fanck, the primary director, films on icebergs and ice floes. The actors often fall into the ice water. Leni Riefenstahl has to

leave the set early because her bladder colic becomes unbearable.

DIRECTOR

59 During the filming of *Tiefland*, 1940 in Krün. She works on this film, with interruptions caused by the war, until 1954.

THE BLUE LIGHT
1932

60 Publicity still as Junta. In the first film she directs herself, Leni Riefenstahl achieves internation-

al recognition, is awarded a silver medal at the first Biennale in Venice and establishes a third career: as a director. She not only plays the leading role but also produces and edits the film herself. She writes the script together with the Jewish film theorist Béla Balázs.

61 Junta flees from the villagers. The film is not made in the studio – as was the usual practice then – but on location in Ticino and the Dolomites.

62-63 After a long search for

nonprofessional actors, she finds mountain farmers from the then still secluded Sarn Valley near Bolzano. The farmers, who had never left their village, take part in the film only after completing the annual harvest.

64 Photograph of the film work in the Dolomites. The crew makes several test shots for many of the scenes to see whether the lighting can be improved.

65-66 The Viennese painter Vigo (Mathias Wieman) falls in love with the shy Junta.

67 Here Junta jumps over a deep chimney.

68 Junta climbs without ropes on the sheer face. The film stock, developed especially for the shooting, makes scenes photographed during the day look like night shots.

69 The director has special portrait lenses sent from Hollywood, where the close-up shot was perfected.

70 In the waterfall's spray. This scene is filmed near Foroglio in

63   64   65   66

67   68   69   70   71

TRIUMPH OF THE WILL

72   73   74   75   76

77   78   79

the Maggia Valley in Ticino, Switzerland.

71 In the crystal grotto. The lighting makes the polished shards of glass seem to glow.

TRIUMPH OF THE WILL
1935

72 Directing in Nuremberg. After seeing *The Blue Light* Hitler personally seeks out the director to make a film about the party rally of 1933. The work on the film is hampered by the party because Leni Riefenstahl is a

woman and not even a party member. All that results is the short film *Victory of Faith*. But Hitler insists that she make the film for the party rally in 1934 as well and he gives it the title *Triumph of the Will*.

73 On the Luitpold Grove Leni Riefenstahl photographs the mass parades from an especially constructed elevator attached to a 125-foot-tall flagpole.

74 March on the Luitpold Grove. The architect Albert Speer stages the Nuremberg

party rallies and designs the buildings for the party rally area.

75 The camera crew experiments with innovative shots and perspectives. Several scenes, for example, are filmed on roller skates and with a camera moving on rails. With this work she establishes a new style for documentary films.

76 Hitler's arrival in Nuremberg.

77 March through Nuremberg.

78 The enthusiastic crowd on the

street welcomes Hitler. As many as a million people travel to Nuremberg for the party rallies.

79 Leni Riefenstahl is the only woman with official order to do an artistic film on the party rally.

OLYMPIA
1938

80-81 The first part, *Festival of the People*, opens with the columns of the Parthenon. American filmmakers include the *Olympia* films among the ten best films of all time.

82-84 The crew films some of the antique statues in the Glyptothek in Munich.

85-86 The *Discobolus of Myron* and decathlete Erwin Huber as a discus thrower. The dissolve symbolizes the transition from antiquity to the present.

87 Cameraman Willy Zielke films this temple dancer on the Kurisch Spit.

88 The lighting of the Olympic flame is reshot on the Baltic Sea using a torch bearer because the

OLYMPIA

80

81

82

83

84

85

86

87

88

89

90

91

92

93

94

95

96

97

98

location shots in Greece are spoiled by cars and motorcycles. The famous set designer Robert Herlth constructs a faithful copy of a fragment of a column for this scene.

89 The torch bearer Anatol.

90 In 1936 a relay team of 3,000 runners carries the Olympic flame to Berlin.

91-92 Entry of the Olympic teams into the Berlin stadium: the men from India and the women from Britain.

93 The director with the cameraman Guzzi Lantschner during the preparations for the film.

94 Discussing the direction; the director of production Walter Traut (left) at the front. She heads a crew of 42 cameramen; with assistants, chauffeurs and directors of photography, the crew includes 150 members.

95 Jesse Owens, USA, is the most successful athlete and the star of the Games. She meets him again at the Olympic Games in Munich in 1972.

96 Cameraman Leo de Laforgue with his miniature camera at the start of a 100-meter race. Each cameraman specializes in filming particular events and is given individual training beforehand.

97 Glenn Morris, USA, sets a world record in the decathlon and wins the gold medal.

98 The winner of the marathon, Kitei Son, Japan, with a wreath of oak leaves. Leni Riefenstahl films every victory ceremony in a different way.

99 Leni Riefenstahl with cameraman Walter Frentz in one of the six filming pits at the Berlin stadium that the stadium officials permitted only after a long struggle.

100-103 Men's high jump: Thurber, USA; Albritton, USA; Asakuma, Japan; the gold medal winner Johnson, USA.

104 The shadows of the marathon runners. During training the runners carry a wire basket with a miniature camera that they can trigger themselves. This allows

the viewer to follow the race from the runner's point of view.

105 The prologue of the second section, *Festival of Beauty,* shows the athletes at the Olympic village, running through the forest.

106 In the sauna.

107-108 Rowing final, here showing Mario Checacci of the Italian eight, and helmsman Robert G. Moch of the US eight. These shots are filmed in advance during the training sessions and later dubbed with sound from the events.

99

100

101

102

103

104

105

106

107

108

109

110

111

109 Leni Riefenstahl with cameraman Hans Ertl.

110 American gymnasts during their free exercises. The scene is filmed from below so that the gymnasts stand out against the sky and present a clear pictorial composition.

111 On the balance beam.

112 The German dodecathlete Waldemar Steffens on the vaulting horse.

113 The gold medal English six-

meter boat, before the wind. The regatta takes place in Kiel and is filmed by Walter Frentz.

114-115 Hans Ertl takes the first underwater shots used in sports photography with a camera he developed himself. With his camera, he dives alongside the divers.

116 The high diving is the final climax of the second section. The divers are filmed using three cameras running at different speeds.

117-119 Dorothy Poynton-Hill, USA, winner in the women's

high diving; Marshall Wayne, USA, gold medal winner in the men's high diving; Marjorie Gestring, USA, winner of the three-meter diving. At first the names of the athletes are mentioned; then the shooting speed decreases until the divers in slow motion seem like birds in flight.

120 Sunset.

121 "The Cathedral of Light" above the stadium concludes the Olympic Games and the film. It was devised by Albert Speer and

is formed by the beams of 130 antiaircraft lights.

122 During the 129 competitions in the Olympic Games, 1.3 million feet of film are shot, sorted, and edited. The director works intensively for two years in all to create a film that will be interesting to audiences, even nonathletes, of all nations.

TIEFLAND
1940–1954

123 Leni Riefenstahl as the Gypsy dancer Martha. The di-

rector plays the leading role and also produces and edits the film.

124 The Berlin zoologist Dr. Bernhard Grzimek trains several wolves for the film.

125 Franz Eichberger as the shepherd Pedro, filmed near the Rosengarten massif in the Dolomites. Leni Riefenstahl happens upon him while skiing and has him take diction lessons for the film.

126 The dangerous scene showing the fight with the wolf is

112   113   114   115

116   117   118   119

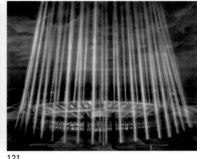

120   121   122

TIEFLAND

123   124   125   126

played by Franz Eichberger without a double. An anesthetic injection "kills" the wolf.

127 Several mountain farmers from the Sarn Valley again work as extras for the film.

128 In Krün in the Karwendel Mountains, a village, a castle, and a mill are built for the film in autumn 1940; they soon become a tourist attraction. Because of the war, the shooting cannot take place in Spain as planned.

129 Martha dances in the inn.

15 years after concluding her dance career, Leni Riefenstahl rehearses her dance scenes with Harald Kreutzberg.

130-131 Bernhard Minetti plays Martha's lover, a hard-hearted Spanish landowner.

132 A reconstruction of the courtyard of the castle is built in the studio by the set designers Isabella Ploberger and Erich Grave.

133+135 In a fight over Martha, Pedro strangles Don Sebastian.

134 The farmers watch the life and death struggle between the shepherd and the hated landowner Don Sebastian.

127   128   129

130   131   132

133   134   135

FOTOGRAFIN PHOTOGRAPHER   THE LAST OF THE NUBA

136   137   138

PHOTOGRAPHER

136 Between 1962 and 1977 she travels to Sudan several times, living with her Nuba friends and learning their language. Her photographs of the Nuba garner international attention in the 1970s. In all she publishes three books of photographs on Africa.

THE LAST OF THE NUBA

137 Two lyre players in the village of Tadoro. Music is one of the passions of the Mesakin Quissayr Nuba.

138 A tobacco field near Tadoro. The Nuba fields are several miles from the village. In addition to tobacco, they plant sorghum, peanuts, and beans.

139 In the *seribe* (herd camp). Here the young men live in isolation from the village community and prepare for the traditional wrestling matches.

140 During the harvest in the village of Tadoro. The men thresh the sorghum in threshing areas that the women prepare for that purpose.

141 To make it visibly evident that they are living in the *seribe*, the young warriors cover themselves with white ash. This is a religious ritual for the Nuba, but the ash also serves to cool their skin and protect it from the sun and pests.

142 On the way to the wrestling festival. The calabashes that the Nuba warriors wear at the waist are decoration for the festival. The larger the calabash, the greater the warrior's reputation. If his calabash breaks, his defeat is assured.

143 Nuba wrestlers in the village of Tolabe. The wrestlers of various Nuba villages come together to prepare for the traditional festival.

144 Wrestling. The best wrestlers are decorated with tails, which put them at a significant disadvantage. The victor is all the more celebrated for that reason.

145 The best wrestler – here, Natu – carries the flag of his village during the festival. The remainder of the time it is kept

with other preparations for the festival in a house in the village dedicated to this purpose.

146 Funeral for a Nuba warrior killed by a poisonous snake. His friends wait for the beginning of the funeral, at which they will sacrifice cows.

147 The close relatives and intimate friends of the deceased dust themselves with white ash for the funeral.

148 Wake. The mother of the dead warrior sings the lament.

139

140

141

142

143

144

145

146

147

148

149

150

His friends wrap him in a white cloth for the burial.

149 A man who is holding the wake has painted a skeleton on his body with ash. Friends of the deceased hold a wake during the funeral to protect the dead man from evil spirits.

150 A night photograph of Nuba warriors. Blowing into a kudu horn signals the end of the matches, and the exhausted young warriors wait for the march home. In 1973 the photographer's first collection of

photographs is published: *The Last of the Nuba* (English edition 1974).

THE PEOPLE OF KAU

151 A Nuba woman from Kau is tattooed. The skin is raised with a thorn so that an incision can be made with a knife. The procedure lasts several days and is extremely painful.

152 View of the village of Kau, which lies some 120 miles east of the villages of the Mesakin Quissayr Nuba. In winter 1975

the photographer lives with the southeast Nuba for five months and she devotes her second volume of photographs, *The People of Kau* (1976), to their rituals.

153 The village square of Kau, then still untouched by Arab and Western civilization. The language of the villagers differs from that of the Mesakin Quissayr Nuba.

154 In an article in *ZEIT-magazin* in 1998 Leni Riefenstahl chooses this portrait of

Jamila as her photograph of the century.

155 The Nuba men of Kau paint their faces very artistically. No mask resembles any other. Only the young warriors are allowed to paint themselves; the pigments are obtained from, among other things, coal dust and ground shells.

156-158 After the photographer shows the Nuba of Kau her first collection of photographs of the Mesakin Quissayr Nuba, many of the men allow her to photo-

graph them with their faces painted in various ways.

159 Shrill screams of the men from the cliffs announce a fighting contest.

160 The black paint of the Nuba warrior is meant to frighten the enemy.

161-162 *Zuar,* the knife duels of the Nuba of Kau. The warriors wear a round, heavy double-edge knife on one arm. Any kind of blow is permitted. The judges watch the matches closely and

THE PEOPLE OF KAU

151   152   153

154   155   156   157

158   159   160   161

162   163   164   165

stop the men before the injuries become fatal.

163–165 The dance festival *nyertun* traditionally takes place after the knife duels. *Nyertun* is a love dance in which unmarried girls are permitted to choose a husband. The girls slowly approach the men, who are staring at the ground. At the sound of a particular drum beat, each of the naked girls places her right leg on the shoulder of the man she has chosen. This is the signal that he may spend the night with her and marry her if she chooses.

TAUCHERIN **DIVER**

166

167

168

169

170

171

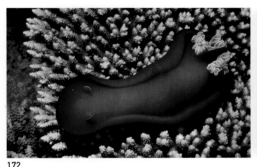
172

173

DIVER

166 Leni Riefenstahl as an underwater photographer around 1980. At the age of 71, while snorkeling in the Indian Ocean, she discovers the underwater world for the first time. She learns to dive, and in her fifth career she publishes two well-received volumes of photographs, *Coral Gardens* (1978) and *Wonders under Water* (English edition 1991).

167 Spiral thread corals, Maldive Islands. To join the diving class she changes her birth year from 1902 to 1922. Everyone is that much more surprised when she reveals her secret at the celebration for those who passed the test. At 98 she is now considered the oldest diver in the world.

168 Sheath squirts, sponges and small corals, Maldive Islands. With her life partner and colleague, Horst Kettner, she has been traveling for more than 25 years to various diving sites in the world, including the Maldive Islands, Indonesia, and Papua New Guinea.

169 Tentacles of the giant sea anemone, *Stoichactis,* Turks Islands, British West Indies, Caribbean. The tentacles are densely covered with stingers.

170 Crocodile fish, Red Sea.

171 Colorful sponges, sea squirts and small branching hydroids, Maldive Islands. Underwater, Leni Riefenstahl photographs with a special reflex camera that makes it possible to see the entire viewfinder, despite the waterproof housing and the diving mask. The feeling of weightlessness under water frees her from the intense pain from which she has suffered since a skiing accident.

172 Spanish dancer, sea slugs, a nocturnal snail, Red Sea. The destruction of the underwater world has led Leni Riefenstahl to become a member of Greenpeace – the first time in her life she has joined any organization.

173 Feather star, Maldive Islands. During their many dives Leni Riefenstahl and Horst Kettner have also shot film. Excerpts from the planned film on the undersea world can be seen in Ray Müller's prize-winning documentary *The Wonderful, Horrible Life of Leni Riefenstahl* (1993).

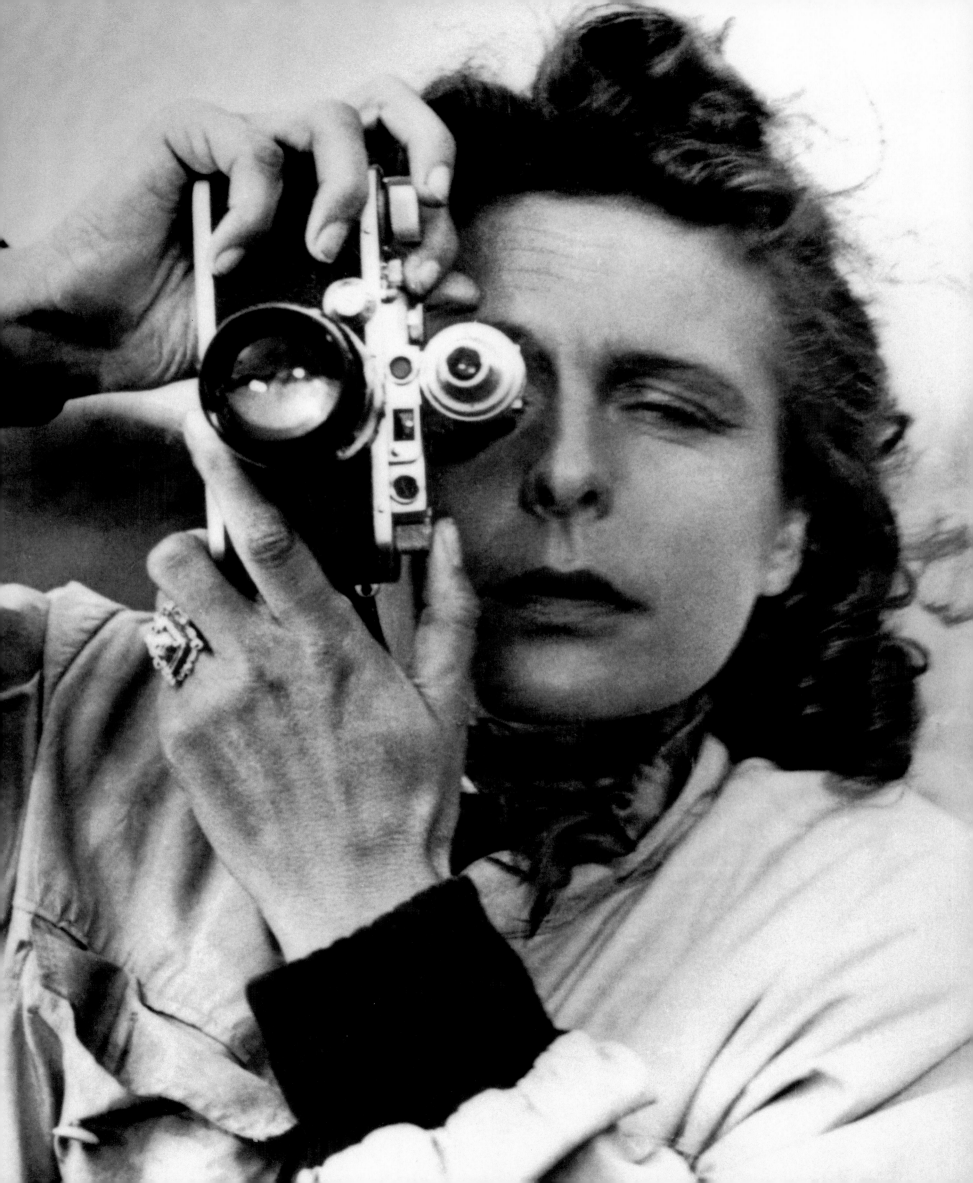

FILMS WITH AND BY
LENI RIEFENSTAHL

CREDITS

D (Director); **DG** (Directorial Guidance); **AD** (Assistant Director); **PC** (Production Company); **P** (Producer); **EP** (Executive Producer); **C** (Camera); **AC** (Assistant Camera); **SP** (Still Photographer); **SC** (Special Camera/Special Effects); **E** (Editor); **SW** (Screenwriter); **LM** (Literary Model); **S** (Sound); **SEn** (Sound Engineer); **SEd** (Sound Editor); **Dia** (Dialogue); **DiaC** (Dialogue Coach); **M** (Music); **Sets** (Sets); **Co** (Costumes); **Ma** (Masks); **Scul** (Sculptor); **Con** (Consultant) **Dist** (Distribution); **SD** (Shooting Dates); **EL** (Exterior Locations); **Stu** (Studio); **Prem** (Premiere); **R** (Rating); **Aw** (Awards) **A** (Actor); **N** (Narrator)

THE HOLY MOUNTAIN –
A HEROIC SONG FROM A TOWERING WORLD OF HEIGHTS
DER HEILIGE BERG –
EIN HELDENLIED AUS RAGENDER HÖHENWELT 1926

Silent film, b/w
118 minutes

The film tells the dramatic story of a love triangle in the Alps. It begins with the dance of Diotima (Leni Riefenstahl) in the foam-flecked waves of the stormy sea. A tour brings the dancer to the mountains, where she will present her stage act at a hotel. Young Vigo (Ernst Petersen) and his older friend (Luis Trenker, whose character is unnamed), both mountain climbers, see the dancer and both fall in love with her. Vigo, the more adventurous of the two, immediately seeks contact with Diotima, while the older man timidly refrains from any attempt to approach her, withdrawing instead into the isolation of the winter mountains. Fascinated by the beauty of the mountain landscape, Diotima wanders as if intoxicated through the mountains, where she meets the older man at a cabin; they fall in love with each other. Diotima nevertheless continues her friendship with the dashing Vigo, whom she encourages during a "fox hunt" (playful chase) on skis. Following this descent at breakneck speeds, she rewards him for his victory by allowing him to rest his head in her lap; her future fiancé sees this gesture, which is really more motherly than intimate. The two friends quarrel. Jealous, the older man challenges Vigo to a dangerous climbing tour in the icy mountains and then causes Vigo to fall from an overhang. At the last moment, however, the older man regains his senses and grabs the safety rope; it takes all his strength to hold on to Vigo's rope. While Diotima is warning the mountain rescue and then searching for the lost men herself, the two men wait out an icy night but then fall to their deaths in the morning mist. The death scene is superimposed with the vision of a gigantic ice cathedral in which Diotima and her fiancé ceremoniously approach the altar, where, to his horror, she turns from him in pain and disappears.

D Arnold Fanck; PC Universum-Film AG (UFA), Cultural Division, Berlin; C Sepp Allgeier, Helmar Lerski, Hans Schneeberger; on location: Arnold Fanck and the Freiburg School; AC Albert Benitz, Kurt Neubert; E Arnold Fanck; SW Arnold Fanck; Hans Schneeberger; M Edmund Meisel; Sets Leopold Blonder; Scul Karl Böhm
Dist Parufamet; Transit-Film, Munich; SD January 1925 until July 1926; EL Lenzerheide, Sils Maria, Interlaken, Zermatt, Feldberg, Arlberg, Helgoland; Prem 17 December 1926 at the UFA-Palast am Zoo, Berlin
A Leni Riefenstahl, Luis Trenker, Ernst Petersen, Hannes Schneider, Friedrich Schneider, Frida Richard, Edmund Meisel
Silent film, b/w, 10,179 feet, 9 acts, 118 minutes, 35 mm, 1:1.33

Notes At the film's premiere Leni Riefenstahl gives her final public dance performance. On the cinema's stage she presents "The Unfinished", a dance she choreographed herself to music by Franz Schubert. The film "The Holy Mountain" is very successful at the box office and impresses the public in particular with its unusual shots of the landscape and clouds. It is also shown under the title "The Sacred Mountain".

THE GREAT LEAP –
AN IMPROBABLE BUT HAPPY STORY
DER GROSSE SPRUNG –
EINE UNWAHRSCHEINLICHE, ABER LUSTIGE GESCHICHTE 1927

Silent film, b/w
112 minutes

A film about the goatherd Gita (Leni Riefenstahl) who lives with six younger siblings and her favorite goat, Pippa, in a small village in the Alps. The athletic Gita, a natural mountaineer, climbs barefoot to escape her somewhat maladroit admirer Toni (Luis Trenker), when they go hiking together. She waits for him on a cliff top and showers him with ridicule when he finally conquers the peak. Michael Treuherz (Hans Schneeberger), the hypochondriac heir to a fortune, visits the mountains with his servant (Paul Graetz) in order to recuperate from the stress of city life. His doctor has prescribed "mountain climbing and a bit of marriage." Ambitious but clumsy, he practices hiking and rock climbing. When he falls into a rushing stream, Gita finds him and frees him by biting through his rope. Treuherz learns to ski, assisted first by the clumsy Toni and then by Gita, who offers herself as the prize for a ski race. Treuherz takes part in the race in a suit inflated with air, which is meant to protect him from his frequent falls. Even Pippa the goat rides along on skis; and Treuherz's servant prepares a surprise meal on the mountain slope. The race ends in Treuherz' victory. He has now won Gita, and after a series of images of the changing landscape in various seasons, the film ends with a shot of Gita, Treuherz, and their young son coming out of the cabin.

D Arnold Fanck; PC Universum-Film AG (UFA), Berlin; EP Ernst Krieger; C Sepp Allgeier, Hans Schneeberger, Albert Benitz, Richard Angst, Kurt Neubert, Charles Métain; SP Hans Casparius; E Arnold Fanck; SW Arnold Fanck; M Werner Richard Heymann; Sets Erich Czerwonski
Dist Parufamet; SD May to November 1927; EL Dolomites, Arlberg ski region; Prem 20 December 1927 at the UFA-Palast am Zoo, Berlin
A Leni Riefenstahl, Luis Trenker, Hans Schneeberger, Paul Graetz
Silent film, b/w, 9,614 feet, 7 acts, 112 minutes, 35 mm, 1:1.33

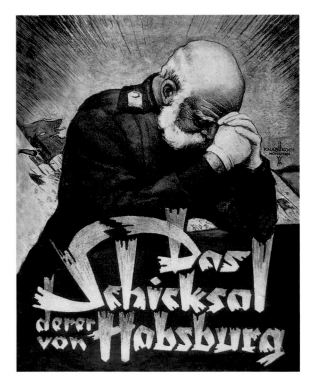

THE DESTINY OF THE HAPSBURGS —
THE TRAGEDY OF AN EMPIRE
DAS SCHICKSAL DERER VON HABSBURG —
DIE TRAGÖDIE EINES KAISERREICHES 1928

Silent film, b/w

The film tells the melodramatic mix-up of love at the imperial Austrian court at the turn of the century. It centers around the two heirs of the Empress Sissi (Erna Morena) and Emperor Francis Joseph I (Fritz Spira) – Crown Prince Rudolf (Alfons Fryland) and his cousin Franz Ferdinand (Willi Hubert). To please his father, the emperor, Rudolf marries Belgian Princess Stefanie (Maly Delschaft). At first, contrary to all expectation, the couple is happy, but they separate when the birth of a daughter rather than the hoped-for male heir leads to a quarrel between Rudolf and his father. Rudolf falls in love with the Baroness Mary Vetsera (Leni Riefenstahl). His wife discovers the relationship, surprises the lovers at breakfast together and strikes the baroness with a riding crop. The emperor obliges his son to return to Stefanie. When saying farewell to the baroness, Rudolf learns that she is expecting his child. The lovers' only way out is a dual suicide. Rudolf's cousin Franz Ferdinand becomes heir to the throne. The imperial family is plunged into terminal decline. Empress Sissi is murdered in Geneva, Franz Ferdinand marries his lover, Countess Chotek (Minje van Gooten), who is beneath his rank and has to renounce any claim to the throne or hereditary titles for herself or her descendants, and in June 1914 the couple is assassinated in Sarajevo, precipitating the outbreak of World War I. It is a war the emperor will not see out. Charles I succeeds him, but following the revolution of 1918 is forced to leave the country.

D Rolf Raffé; AD Rolf Eckbauer; PC Essem-Film Produktion, Berlin; EP Leo Meyer; C Marius Holdt; SW Max Ferner; Sets Arthur Berger
Dist Berlin and the east: Star Film, Berlin; Rhineland, Westphalia, Saar region: Rheinische Film, Cologne; central Germany: Siegel Monopolfilm, Dresden; southern Germany: Leofilm, Munich; northern Germany: Nordfilm, Hamburg; EL Schönbrunn Castle near Vienna; Prem 16 November 1928 at the Waterloo-Theater, Hamburg
A Fritz Spira, Erna Morena, Maly Delschaft, Leni Riefenstahl, Alfons Fryland, Franz Kammauf, Willi Hubert, Ernst Recniczek, Albert Kersten, Paul Askonas, Ferry Lukacs, Irene Kraus, Carmen Cartellieri, Alice Roberte, Minje van Gooten
Silent film, b/w, c. 7,900 feet

Notes The film is lost; the plot has been taken from a surviving program book. The popular story of Crown Prince Rudolf and Baroness Mary Vetsera was the subject of many films, among others "Mayerling" (1968) by Terence Young, with Omar Sharif and Catherine Deneuve.

THE WHITE HELL OF PITZ PALU
DIE WEISSE HÖLLE VOM PIZ PALÜ 1929

Silent film, b/w   Sound version, 1935 b/w
127 minutes   92 minutes

A mountain drama on the Bernina massif. When Maria (Mizzi Götzel), the wife of Dr. Johannes Krafft (Gustav Diessl), dies after falling into a glacier crevasse at Pitz Palu, Krafft becomes obsessed with the mountains and hikes alone through the Bernina Alps, where he becomes a legend as the "Spirit of the Mountain." He meets the couple Maria Majoni (Leni Riefenstahl) and Hans Brandt (Ernst Petersen) in the Diavolezza shelter, just as they are reading the legend about him in the guest book. The young woman and Krafft are strongly attracted to each other. The three, along with the mountain guide Otto Spring (Christian Klucker), spend the night in the cabin. When Krafft sets out alone the next morning to climb the north face of Pitz Palu, Hans, now jealous, sets off after him. Maria follows Hans, and a group of students from Zurich also heads for the peak. During a rapid and dangerous ascent, Hans, who is an inexperienced climber, falls over an ice overhang. Krafft and Maria are able to pull him up, but he breaks a leg in the accident. They stay with him and wait on a ledge for help while the group of students goes on. Stormy weather approaches; the students are struck by an avalanche. Otto Spring calls out the mountain rescue team, which sets out at night and finds the students but not Maria, Hans, and Krafft. During the three days they spend waiting, Krafft tries to ease Hans's pain and anxiety. He gives him warm clothing and ties him to the rock for safety when Hans is struck by a fit of madness. Ernst Udet sets out in his plane to search for the missing hikers, locates them on the ledge, and indicates the site to Otto Spring and the mountain rescue team. In the meanwhile, however, Krafft has tried to climb down without ropes and has frozen to death in the attempt. The rescue team succeeds in freeing Maria and Hans from the ice, and they narrowly escape death.

D Arnold Fanck, Georg Wilhelm Pabst; AD Mark Sorkin; PC Henry R. Sokal-Film, Berlin; P Henry Richard Sokal; EP Henry Richard Sokal; C Sepp Allgeier, Richard Angst, Hans Schneeberger; SP Hans Casparius; E Arnold Fanck, Hermann Haller; SW Arnold Fanck, Ladislaus Vajda; based on an idea by Arnold Fanck; M silent film: Willy Schmidt-Gentner; sound version: Giuseppe Becce; Sets Ernö Metzner
Dist AAFA-Film, special distribution Berlin; Goldeck; SD January to June 1929; EL Morteratsch Glacier, Pitz Palu; Stu Grunewald Studio, Berlin; Prem Silent film: 11 October 1929 at various cinemas in Vienna; 22 October 1929 at the Universum-Lichtspiele, Mannheim; 15 November 1929 at the UFA-Palast am Zoo, Berlin; 13 December 1929 at the Marivaux-Pathé, Paris; 5 September 1930 Rialto, London; sound version: 23 December 1935 at the UFA-Pavillon am Nollendorfplatz, Berlin; 26 September 1930 New York; R didactic film, artistic
A Leni Riefenstahl, Gustav Diessl, Ernst Petersen, Ernst Udet, Mizzi Götzel, Christian Klucker
Silent film 1929: b/w, 3,330 m, 7 acts, 127 minutes, 35 mm, 1:1.33
Sound version 1935: b/w, 8,230 feet, 92 minutes, 35 mm, 1:1.33

Notes The film is, along with Fritz Lang's "Die Frau im Mond" (The Woman in the Moon), one of the most profitable films of the 1929–1930 season in Germany, grossing 2.2 million reichsmarks and drawing international attention to the genre of the mountain film. It is shown in Paris and London. An American sound version produced by Universal Pictures in 1930 becomes the first German film ever to be shown in the US, where it fills the large New York cinema The Roxy. The film is shown also under the title "Prisoners of the Mountain". For the French market Leni Riefenstahl edits a shorter version, and in 1935 a shortened sound version is released in Germany. The remake "Föhn" (1950) is filmed by Rolf Hansen with the actors Hans Albers, Liselotte Pulver, and Adrian Hoven in the studio. For the 1997 Berlin Film Festival a restored version of the silent film "The White Hell of Pitz Palu" is produced and shown to music by Ashley Irwin.

STORM OVER MONT BLANC
STÜRME ÜBER DEM MONTBLANC 1930

Sound film, b/w
110 minutes

The film tells of a love story in the mountains. Meteorological observer Hannes (Sepp Rist) lives a solitary but satisfied life on Mont Blanc. His only contact with the world is through the radio on which he hears his friend Walter (Mathias Wieman) play the organ. In the valley lives Hella Armstrong (Leni Riefenstahl), who, together with her father (Friedrich Kayssler), an astronomer from northern Germany, runs the observatory. Hella, who loves to ski, takes part in a "fox hunt" and escapes the men chasing her by climbing into an airplane with Ernst Udet. While flying over Mont Blanc they wave to Hannes. After she returns, Hella and her father visit the meteorological station, and Hella and Hannes fall in love. During their climb to the measuring station, Hella's father falls to his death. Hannes consoles her and advises her to visit his sick friend Walter, who will take her mind off her grief. Meanwhile, Hannes prepares for a relief to take over at the weather station. Hella takes care of Walter and she praises him to the skies in a letter to Hannes. Hannes misinterprets the letter and thinks the two are having an affair. Jealous, he decides to spend another year on Mont Blanc. A storm approaches. When Hannes loses his gloves on the mountain, his hands freeze. Now he can no longer make a fire, so he risks his life descending during the storm without skis. Cracks in the glacier force him to turn back, but the storm has almost destroyed the weather station. However, he is still able to send a mayday message by radio, which Hella picks up at the observatory. With a rescue team she sets off for Mont Blanc, but Udet arrives at the weather station first and is able to build a fire for Hannes.

D Arnold Fanck; **PC** AAFA-Film (Tobis); **EP** Henry Richard Sokal; **C** Hans Schneeberger, Richard Angst, Sepp Allgeier; pilot of the camera plane: Claus von Suchotzky; **E** Arnold Fanck; **SW** Arnold Fanck, Carl Mayer; **SEn** Emil Specht, Hans Grimm, Erich Lange; **SEd** Alwin Elling; **M** Paul Dessau, Otto Firl (uncredited), Edmund Meisel (uncredited); Welte organ: W. A. Harnisch; electronic music: "Trautonium"; phonetic coaching: Herbert Kuchenbuch; **Sets** Leopold Blonder
Dist AAFA-Film, Berlin; **SD** 12 to 30 August 1930; **EL** Arosa, Mont Blanc, Vallot Observatory, Bernina Pass, Babelsberg Observatory; **Stu** UFA Studio Berlin-Tempelhof; **Prem** 25 December 1930 at the Prinzess-Theater, Dresden and the UFA-Theater Schwan, Frankfurt am Main; 19 January 1931 in Vienna; 2 February 1931 at the UFA-Palast am Zoo, Berlin; end of May 1931 at the Pavilion, London; **R** didactic film, artistic
A Leni Riefenstahl, Sepp Rist, Ernst Udet, Mathias Wieman, Friedrich Kayssler, Alfred Beierle, Ernst Petersen; skiers: David Zogg, Beni Führer, Julius Rähmi, Guzzi Lantschner, Otto Lantschner, Benno Leubner, Otto Leubner, Harald Reinl (uncredited), Kurt Reinl, Walter Traut; mountain guides: Braun, Hans Kogler, Josef Gumboldt, Blümel, Luggi Föger
Sound film, b/w, 9,722 feet, 7 acts, 110 minutes, 35 mm, 1:1.33

Note "Storm over Mont Blanc" is also shown under the title "Avalanche" and in a French version as well.

THE WHITE FLAME –
NEW MIRACLES OF THE SNOWSHOE
DER WEISSE RAUSCH –
NEUE WUNDER DES SCHNEESCHUHS 1931

Sound film, b/w
94 minutes

This slapstick comedy is played out in the Austrian Alps. Leni (Leni Riefenstahl), a young woman from Berlin, is spending her winter vacation alone in St. Anton on the Arlberg, where she is learning to jump on skis and wants to participate in the ski race for winter guests. She turns to ski instructor Hannes (Hannes Schneider) for help, who practices with the completely inexperienced city woman every day. Two carpenters from Hamburg (Guzzi Lantschner and Walter Riml) are also trying to learn to ski but they use instructional books instead. Because it is not so simple to translate theory into practice, many hilarious falls ensue. Meanwhile, Leni is also getting help from her small friend Lothar (Lothar Ebersberg) from the village. He shows her how to master a small hill, and with his support she wins the beginners' race. A year later Leni's goals have advanced. In the annual "fox hunt" on skis, she and her former ski instructor Hannes are the "pair of foxes." With many tricks and feints they send their pursuers off on false trails and shake them off again and again. The two carpenters are also back again, and with their unintentional falls they manage to bring the pursuers back on the trail of the foxes. However, despite their sporting prowess the pursuers led by Rudi (Rudi Matt) do not manage to catch Leni and Hannes. It takes little Lothar to accomplish the task by playing a trick on them: he locks the "pair of foxes" in the inn, where their pursuers eventually catch them. Locked in a prison of ice, the skiers end the "fox hunt" with a snowball fight.

D Arnold Fanck; **PC** Henry R. Sokal-Film, Berlin (AAFA-Film, Berlin); **P** Henry Richard Sokal; **EP** Arnold Fanck; **C** Richard Angst, Kurt Neubert (on location), Hans Karl Gottschalk (in the studio); according to Fanck's program text, Benno Leubner as well; **AC** Robert Dahlmeier; **E** Arnold Fanck; **SW** Arnold Fanck; **S** Hans Bittmann, Emil Specht; **SEd** Fritz Seeger; **M** Paul Dessau (conductor), Fritz Goldschmidt (assistant); **Sets** Leopold Blonder
Dist AAFA-Film, Berlin; Goldeck; **SD** 8 to 20 October 1931; **EL** St. Anton and Zürs on the Arlberg; **Stu** Jofa Studios, Berlin-Johannisthal; **Prem** 10 December 1931 at the UFA-Palast am Zoo, Berlin; **R** didactic film, artistic
A Leni Riefenstahl, Hannes Schneider, Guzzi Lantschner, Walter Riml, Rudi Matt, Lothar Ebersberg, Luggi Föger, Josef Gumboldt, Hans Kogler, Benno Leubner, Otto Leubner, Harald Reinl (uncredited)
Sound film, b/w, 8,413 feet, 5 acts, 94 minutes, 35 mm, 1:1.33

Notes This comedy is the first sound film about Alpine ski racing and is considered a cult classic of the sport. More than forty racers perform in it, including the best ski racers of the day: Hannes Schneider, the founder of the famous Arlberg School; Rudi Matt; and the brothers Otto and Guzzi Lantschner. "The White Flame" also ran under the title "White Ecstasy – The Ski Chase", "White Frenzy", "White Rapture" and "White Intoxication". In Germany it was shown also under the title "Skiteufel im Alpenparadies" (Ski Devils in an Alpine Paradise) and in Austria it was called "Sonne über dem Arlberg" (Sun over the Arlberg). In 1952 a sequel was produced, "Karneval in Weiss" (Carnival in White), directed by Hans Albin and Henry Richard Sokal.

THE BLUE LIGHT –
A MOUNTAIN LEGEND FROM THE DOLOMITES
DAS BLAUE LICHT –
EINE BERGLEGENDE AUS DEN DOLOMITEN 1932

Sound film, b/w
86 minutes

The film opens with a frame story. On their honeymoon a young couple passes through the Alpine village of Santa Maria where a picture of a girl is being sold as a souvenir. A close-up of the book that tells her tale leads to the main plot about Junta. The Viennese painter Vigo (Mathias Wieman) travels to Santa Maria, where a dejected mood dominates. Lured by a shimmering blue light that appears on Monte Cristallo on nights with a full moon, many young men from the village have fallen to their deaths while trying to climb the mountain. The villagers blame the girl Junta (Leni Riefenstahl), who lives alone in the mountains. When she comes to the village, she is attacked by the children, and a crystal that Junta found by a waterfall drops from her basket. Young Toni (Beni Führer) tries to save the girl from her pursuers and take her with him, but Junta escapes into the forest. Night falls, the full moon rises, the villagers close their shutters, and the mysterious blue glow appears on the mountain. The next morning the villages discover the corpse of another man who has fallen to his death. They curse the "witch," and when the girl comes to the village, she is chased away, even though Vigo stands up for her. He follows Junta into the forest and falls in love with her. During the next full moon, Junta walks in her sleep to the mountain peak, while Vigo and Toni follow her unnoticed. Toni falls, but Vigo discovers Junta's secret: a grotto filled with rock crystals from which the mysterious glow emanates. After his return, Vigo comes up with a plan to hide the crystals, but Junta does not understand him. To protect her from persecution by the villagers, he tells them about his discovery. The villagers climb the mountain, mine the crystals, and sell them. While the entire village is celebrating, Junta finds a crystal sliver in the forest and guesses what has happened. She climbs up to the grotto, finds it empty, and leaps in despair into the abyss. Vigo finds her body. Junta's portrait on the book of legends fades into the frame story, in which the young married couple now leaves the village.

D Leni Riefenstahl; **PC** Leni Riefenstahl Studio-Film (H. R. Sokal-Film, Berlin); **P** Leni Riefenstahl, Henry Richard Sokal (uncredited); **EP** Walter Traut; **C** Hans Schneeberger; **AC** Heinz von Jaworsky; **SP** Walter Riml; **E** Leni Riefenstahl; **SW** Leni Riefenstahl, Béla Balázs; Hans Schneeberger; **S** Hans Bittmann; **SEd** Hanne Kuyt; **M** Giuseppe Becce; **Sets** Leopold Blonder
Dist AAFA-Film, Berlin (special distribution), Degeto-Kulturfilm, Berlin (from 1938 on), National (after 1945), Taurus (video); **SD** July to September 1931; **EL** Sarentino in the Sarn Valley, Runkelstein Castle, Crozzon in the Brenta mountain group (Dolomites), Maggia Valley in Ticino; **Stu** Studio "Cicero"; **Prem** 24 March 1932 at the UFA-Palast am Zoo, Berlin; 30 October 1932 at the Rialto, London; revival 27 September 1938 at the Kurbel, Berlin; **R** artistic; **Aw** silver medal of the International Film Exhibition 1932 in Venice (Biennale)
A Leni Riefenstahl, Mathias Wieman, Beni Führer, Max Holzboer, Franz Maldacea, Martha Mair, farmers from the Sarn Valley
Original version 1932: Sound film, b/w, 7,688 feet, 9 acts, 86 minutes, 35 mm, 1:1.33
New version 1951: Sound film, b/w, 6,452 feet, 72 minutes, 35 mm, 1:1.33

Notes In the first film she produces herself, Leni Riefenstahl becomes internationally famous as a woman producer, director, inventor of images, and leading actress. At the Venice Film Biennale, which takes place for the first time in 1932, "The Blue Light" wins the silver medal. In France and England the film runs for months in full houses; Charlie Chaplin and Douglas Fairbanks send telegrams from Hollywood to congratulate her. The original negative is lost during the war; as a result the director cuts a new version in 1951 from the unused footage, dropping the frame story. This second version is dubbed afterward and given new music by the composer for the original version, Giuseppe Becce. Leni Riefenstahl considers the new version more successful and more beautiful than the original.

VICTORY OF FAITH –
THE FILM OF THE NATIONAL SOCIALIST PARTY RALLY
SIEG DES GLAUBENS –
DER FILM VOM REICHSPARTEITAG DER NSDAP 1933

Sound film, b/w
64 minutes

Documentary film about the Fifth Party Rally of the National Socialists (Nazi Party), which takes place from 30 August to 3 September 1933 in Nuremberg and represents the first party rally following the Nazi seizure of power on January 1933. The film contains no voice-over or insert titles; rather, the film sequences combine the original sound – marching music, speeches, songs of the National Socialists – with music composed especially for the film.

The order of the sequences: mood shots of early-morning Nuremberg and the structures in the party rally area; politicians and foreign diplomats being welcomed at the train station in Nuremberg and outside the Deutscher Hof hotel; Adolf Hitler's landing at the airport; the welcome ceremony; the party rally being opened; Hitler meeting high-ranking leaders and party members at the Zeppelin Field; columns of standard-bearers marching in through the crowd; the flag being lowered to honor the National Socialist movement's dead; the speech to the Deutsche Arbeitsfront (National Socialist Workers' Organization); various scenes with cheering crowds; a Zeppelin with a swastika flying over the party rally area; Hitler's appearance to Hitler Youth; National Socialist troops parading through the city of Nuremberg; Hitler's speech on the tenth anniversary of the National Socialist movement; the Horst Wessel song.

D Leni Riefenstahl; PC Propaganda Department of the National Socialist Party, Division IV (Film), Berlin; EP Arnold Raether; C Sepp Allgeier, Franz Weihmayr, Walter Frentz, Richard Quaas, Paul Tesch; E Leni Riefenstahl, Waldemar Gaede; S Siegfried Schulze; SEn Siegfried Schulze; SEd Waldemar Gaede; M Herbert Windt
Dist UFA, State Film Authorities of the National Socialists; SD 30 August to 3 September 1933; Prem 1 December 1933 at the UFA-Palast am Zoo, Berlin
Sound film, b/w, 5,760 feet, 64 minutes, 35 mm, 1:1.33

Notes "Victory of Faith" is shot with very little preparation time and is the director's first documentary film. The film department of the National Socialist propaganda ministry, to which Leni Riefenstahl is officially subordinate, hampers the director during the filming, because Hitler chose her even though she is a woman and not a party member. Although the film, made under difficult circumstances, does not please her at all, it is highly praised by the party and the press.

SOS ICEBERG
SOS EISBERG 1933

Sound film b/w
103 minutes

The film tells of the dramatic attempts to rescue the lost participants of an expedition in Greenland. Polar explorer Dr. Carl Lawrence (Gustav Diessl) is missing after violating a prohibition against going out alone. His colleagues, led by Dr. Johannes Brand (Sepp Rist), search for him in vain and then return to Berlin. When notes by the polar explorer are found, the group returns to Greenland to renew the search at the request of his wife, Ellen (Leni Riefenstahl), a pilot. The weather is unfavorable, as the spring thaw is causing the icebergs in Greenland to break loose, and the expedition is forced to advance by leaping from floe to floe. Finally, they locate Lawrence, nearly frozen to death and starving, on a drifting iceberg. By radio they send an SOS, and Ellen sets out immediately by plane. She is able to find the group, but during the water landing, the plane collides with a wall of ice. Now Ellen, too, is caught in the icy wasteland. Without informing the others, Johannes Brand tries to reach the Eskimos alone by swimming through the ice-cold water. Those who remain behind confront extreme challenges: John Dragan (Gibson Gowland) and Fritz Kümmel (Walter Riml) fight to the death; a polar bear attacks; Dr. Jan Matushek (Max Holzboer) goes mad from hunger. The pilot Ernst Udet spots Lawrence and Ellen, who tells Udet to continue to the Eskimo camp. Along the way Udet finds Brand. They persuade the Eskimos to set out in kayaks to find Ellen and Lawrence. On the ship home, the survivors watch as the iceberg on which they had been stranded for days breaks apart and disappears into the sea.

D Arnold Fanck; **AD** Werner Klingler; **PC** Deutsche Universal-Film, Berlin; **P** Paul Kohner (uncredited); **EP** Alfred Stern; **C** Richard Angst, Hans Schneeberger; **AC** Walter Traut, Fritz von Friedl, Heinz von Jaworski, Luggi Föger; **SP** Ferdinand Vogel; **SC** Aerial photographs: Hans Schneeberger; photographs from the plane: Ernst Udet, Franz Schrieck; **E** Hermann Haller, Arnold Fanck; **SW** Arnold Fanck, Fritz Löwe (uncredited), Ernst Sorge (uncredited), Hans Hinrich; **S** Zoltan Kegl; Erich Lange, Werner Klingler, Charles Métain; **SEd** Alice Ludwig; **Dia** Edwin E. Knopf, Friedrich Wolf (assistance), Tom Reed (adaptation); **DiaC** Hans Hinrich; **M** Paul Dessau; **Sets** Fritz Maurischat, Ernst Petersen, Arno Richter; **Ma** Paul Dannenberg; **Con** Fritz Loewe, Ernst Sorge (uncredited), Emmy Langberg
Dist Deutsche Universal-Film, Berlin; Ring; UFA (video); **SD** June to November 1932 in Greenland, early to late May 1933 on the Bernina Pass; **EL** Greenland, Bernina Pass, Berlin; **Stu** Jofa Studios, Berlin-Johannisthal; **Prem** 30 August 1933 at the UFA-Palast am Zoo, Berlin; American version: 23 September 1933 at the Criterion, New York; **R** artistic
A Leni Riefenstahl, Gustav Diessl, Ernst Udet, Gibson Gowland, Sepp Rist, Max Holzboer, Walter Riml, Arthur Grosse, Tommy Thomas; mountain guides: David Zogg, Fritz Steuri, Hans Ertl
Sound film, b/w, 9,273 feet, 6 acts, 103 minutes, 35 mm, 1:1.33

Notes Parallel to the German film, an American version, with minor variations in the plot, is produced for Universal Pictures Corp. under the co-direction of Arnold Fanck and the Hollywood director Tay Garnett. Leni Riefenstahl plays the leading role in the American film as well; her co-stars are Sepp Rist and Rod La Rocque. Sound films produced simultaneously in different languages are common in the early 1930s because producers do not wish to lose access to foreign markets.

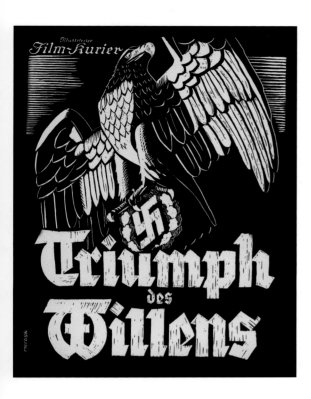

DAY OF FREEDOM! — OUR ARMED FORCES!
TAG DER FREIHEIT! — UNSERE WEHRMACHT! 1935

Sound film, b/w
28 minutes

Documentary film on the army's drills during the Seventh National Socialist Party Rally that takes place from 10 to 16 September 1935 in Nuremberg. The film contains no commentary but consists of original sound and film music composed especially for it.

TRIUMPH OF THE WILL
TRIUMPH DES WILLENS 1935

Sound film, b/w
114 minutes

Documentary film on the Sixth National Socialist Party Rally in Nuremberg held from 4 to 10 September 1934, under the slogan "Party Rally of Unity." Again, the film has no voice-over and the soundtrack consists of the sound from the events combined with original film music. The sequences: flight through the clouds; Hitler landing with the plane; ride through the city; evening concert in front of the Deutscher Hof hotel; images setting the atmosphere of morning in the city; scenes at the camps of the young participants in the party rally; parade of groups in peasant dress; Hitler greeting the Deutsche Arbeitsfront; Rudolf Hess opening the party rally; various speakers, whose last names are indicated on insert titles, including Alfred Rosenberg and Joseph Goebbels; roll call of the Voluntary Workforce on the Zeppelin Field; night speech by SA leader Viktor Lutze, illuminated by campfires and fireworks; the Hitler Youth in the stadium the following day; roll call of the Political Leaders of National Socialist Organizations on the Zeppelin Field; the march of SA and SS troops into the Luitpold Arena; Hitler, Himmler, and Lutze stepping from the arena; the arrival of the standard-bearers with march music; the consecration of the standards with the "flag of blood"; the parade of the National Socialist Organizations with the army through the streets of Nuremberg; Hitler's closing speech in the Luitpold Hall; the march of the SA from the hall; National Socialist hymns.

Notes According to estimates, 180,000 viewers in the area that would later correspond to West Germany saw the film in the week following the premiere. The film earns 200,000 reichsmarks, which makes it the sixth most profitable film of 1935–1936. The film is accompanied by the book "Hinter den Kulissen des Reichsparteitags-Films" (Behind the Scenes of the Party Rally Film), with a text that Ernst Jäger, editor in chief of "Film-Kurier", wrote for the advertising department of UFA. After World War II "Triumph of the Will" is rated a "restricted film" and may thus only be shown together with an introduction in film clubs or for scholarly purposes. The director is accused of having significantly increased, by means of this film, the emotional bond of the Germans to Hitler and the National Socialists. "Triumph of the Will" is one of the most-discussed German films of all time. Its montage of images creates an intensity that was unsurpassed in documentary films of the time. Filmmakers have repeatedly borrowed the camera positions that epitomize "Triumph of the Will", including such Hollywood directors as Paul Verhoeven in "Starship Troopers" (1997) and George Lucas in "Star Wars: Episode I" (1999).

Day of Freedom! – Our Armed Forces!
D Leni Riefenstahl; **PC** Reichsparteitag-Film (Leni Riefenstahl Studio-Film, Berlin); **EP** Leni Riefenstahl; **C** Willy Zielke, Guzzi Lantschner, Walter Frentz, Hans Ertl, Kurt Neubert, Albert Kling; **M** Peter Kreuder; **E** Leni Riefenstahl
Dist UFA-Filmverleih; **Prem** 30 December 1935 at the UFA-Palast am Zoo, Berlin; **R** artistically and politically significant
Notes The film comes about because the director did not want to include the army drills from the previous year in "Triumph of the Will" since they were filmed during poor weather. But General Walter von Reichenau insisted strongly on the shots because 1934 was the first year in which the army participated in the party rally. As a compromise, she proposed that a separate film about the army be shot the following year. The film is distributed as short "army didactic film". In 1936 a 16-mm version of 991 feet is produced.
Sound film, b/w, 2,476 feet, 28 minutes, 35 mm, 1:1.33

Triumph of the Will
D Leni Riefenstahl; **AD** Erna Peters, Guzzi Lantschner, Otto Lantschner, Walter Prager; **PC** Reichsparteitag-Film (Leni Riefenstahl Studio-Film, Berlin); NSDAP, Commerce Authority of Party Rally Film; **EP** Leni Riefenstahl; **C** Sepp Allgeier, Karl Attenberger, Werner Bohne, Walter Frentz, Hans Gottschalk, Werner Hundhausen, Herbert Kebelmann, Albert Kling, Franz Koch, Herbert Kutschbach, Paul Lieberenz, Richard Nickel, Walter Riml, Arthur von Schwertführer, Karl Vaß, Franz Weihmayr, Siegfried Weinmann, Karl Wellert; **AC** Sepp Ketterer, Wolfgang Hart, Peter Haller, Kurt Schulz, Eugen Oskar Bernhard, Richard Kandler, Hans Bühring, Richard Böhm, Erich Stoll, Josef Koch, Otto Jäger, August Beis, Hans Wittmann, Wolfgang Müller, Hans (Heinz) Linke, Erich Küchler, Ernst Kunstmann, Erich Grohmann, Wilhelm Schmidt; **SP** Rolf Lantin; photographic revision: Gisela Lindeck-Schneeberger; **SC** Aerial photographs: the team of Svend Noldan, Fritz Brunsch, Hans Noack; **E** Leni Riefenstahl; **SW** Leni Riefenstahl; **S** Siegfried Schulz, Ernst Schütz; **SEd** Bruno Hartwich, Alice Ludwig; **M** Herbert Windt; march music: the band of Adolf Hitler's personal guard; **Sets** Albert Speer; structures for the film: Councilor Brugmann, with the architect Seegy
Dist UFA-Filmverleih; **SD** 4 to 10 September 1934; **Prem** 28 March 1935 at the UFA-Palast am Zoo, Berlin; **R** politically and artistically significant, didactic; **Aw** National Film Prize 1934–1935; International Film Festival Venice 1935: Coppa dell'Istituto Nazionale LUCE; Medaille d'or and Grand Prix of France 1937
Sound film, b/w, 10,198 feet, 114 minutes, 35 mm, 1:1.33

OLYMPIA PART I FESTIVAL OF THE PEOPLE
OLYMPIA TEIL 1 FEST DER VÖLKER 1938

Sound film, b/w
126 minutes (version approved by the Voluntary Self-Supervision Board of the German Film Industry:
117 minutes)

OLYMPIA PART II FESTIVAL OF BEAUTY
OLYMPIA TEIL 2 FEST DER SCHÖNHEIT 1938

Sound film, b/w
100 Minutes (version approved by the Voluntary Self-Supervision Board of the German Film Industry:
99 minutes)

Documentary film on the 11th Olympic Games, which took place from 1 to 16 August 1936 in Berlin.

Summary of *Festival of the People* (Part I). Prologue: Title sequence of inscriptions carved in stone; images of clouds and fog with music; Acropolis and statues of ancient athletes and goddesses; statue of a disc thrower becomes a living athlete; temple dancers; the lighting of the Olympic flame and the torch relay; map of the route through Europe to Berlin; parade of the arriving teams; Hitler opening the Games; Olympia bell; the Olympic Hymn by Richard Strauss; Olympic flame and sunset fading into the Olympic rings; introduction of the commentators in various languages; the disciplines: discus, javelin, 80-meter hurdles, hammer, 100-meter sprint, high jump, shot put, 800-meter run, triple jump, long jump, 1,500 meters, 10,000 meters, pole vault; 4 x 100-meter relay, 4 x 400-meter relay, marathon. Part I ends with the nighttime parade of the standard-bearers into the stadium.

Festival of Beauty (Part II) also begins with prologue: title sequence; Olympic flag; the lives of the athletes in the Olympic village. The disciplines: gymnastics, sailing, fencing, boxing, modern pentathlon, decathlon, hockey, polo, soccer game between Austria and Italy, 100-meter cycle race, military, rowing, high diving, 200-meter breaststroke, 100-meter freestyle. The conclusion includes the final ceremony, the Olympic stadium lit up at night, the "Cathedral of Light", the Olympic flame, the Olympic flag.

D Leni Riefenstahl; **PC** Olympia-Film, Berlin; **P** Leni Riefenstahl; **EP** Walter Traut, Walter Grosskopf; **C** Hans Ertl (underwater shots and running races), Walter Frentz (sailing, marathon, captive balloon), Guzzi Lantschner (riding, gymnastics, swimming, rowing), Kurt Neubert (slow-motion shots), Hans Scheib (telephoto shots), Willy Zielke (prologue), Leo de Laforgue (shots of the public), among many other cameramen; **SP** Rolf Lantin; **SC** torch run scenes by team of Svend Noldan; **E** Leni Riefenstahl, Max Michel, Johannes Lüdke, Arnfried Heyne, Guzzi Lantschner; **S** Hermann Storr; **SEd** Max Michel, Johannes Lüdke, Arnfried Heyne, Guzzi Lantschner, Wolfgang Brüning, Otto Lantschner; **SEn** Siegfried Schulze; **M** Herbert Windt, Walter Gronostay; **Sets** Robert Herlth; **Con** Josef Schmücker; **N** Paul Laven, Rolf Wernicke, Henri Nannen, Johannes Pagels
Dist Tobis; Müller, Taurus (video); **SD** July/August 1936; **Prem** 20 April 1938 at the UFA-Palast am Zoo, Berlin; **R** artistically and politically significant, culturally significant, for popular education, didactic film; **Aw** National Film Prize 1937–38, International Film Festival Venice 1938: Coppa Mussolini (Best Film), Polar Prize Sweden 1938, Greek Sports Prize 1938; Olympic Gold Medal of the Comité International Olympique 1939; International Film Festival Lausanne 1948: Olympic Diploma
Sound film, b/w, Part I: 11,247 feet, 35 mm, 1:1.33, 126 minutes (version approved by the Voluntary Self-Supervision Board of the German Film Industry: 117 minutes); Part II: 8,928 feet, 35 mm, 1:1.33, 100 minutes (version approved by the Voluntary Self-Supervision Board of the German Film Industry : 99 minutes)

Notes The "Olympia" films were produced in four different language versions: German, English, French, and Italian. At the 1937 Paris World Fair, a film about the making of the "Olympia" films, shot by Otto Lantschner and edited by Rudolf Schaad, wins a gold medal. The "Olympia" films are considered unsurpassed in pictorial aesthetic, and even today are counted among the greatest documentary films on sports. The film critic Richard Corliss, a coeditor of "Time", remarked in 1993: "All televised sport is indebted to 'Olympia'." In 1956 American directors include the "Olympia" films among the ten best films of all times. Other critics, including Susan Sontag, have found a fascist aesthetic in the films and emphasize that at the time of their production, they helped to convey the image of a peace-loving nation to the outside world.

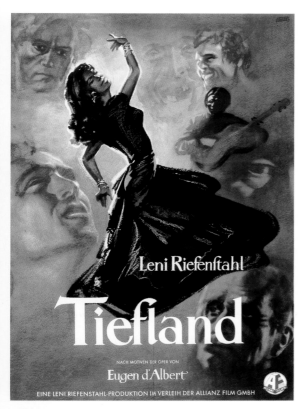

TIEFLAND (LOWLANDS)
TIEFLAND 1940–1954

Sound film, b/w
99 minutes

Nature-loving shepherd Pedro (Franz Eichberger) guards over the herds of Marques Sebastian Roccabruna (Bernhard Minetti) in the mountains. When a wolf attacks his herds, he strangles it with his bare hands. He fetches the price for the wolf's coat from the domineering marques down in the lowlands, who is taking away the water from his tenant farmers in order to water the bulls he raises for bull fighting. Pedro and the marques see the Gypsy Martha (Leni Riefenstahl) dance in a tavern, and both of them fall in love with her. Don Sebastian makes Martha his lover, while Pedro, back with his sheep, can only dream of her. Martha witnesses a confrontation between Don Sebastian and his tenant farmers, who are asking for water. When the marques learns that Martha has given one of his gifts, a valuable chain, to the poor miller's family so that they can pay their rent, he strikes her. She runs to Pedro, but the marques' servants track her down, and she has to return to him. Doña Amelia (Maria Koppenhöfer), the daughter of the rich mayor, would like to marry Don Sebastian, who has lost his wealth. His lawyer (Aribert Wäscher) forces him to marry for money and devises a plan: naive Pedro will marry Martha at the same time, so that she will continue to be available to the marques. Pedro, who is not told about the plan, is happy, and when the villagers mock him during the wedding, he assumes that Martha will not love him. During the night when the two couples are married a storm arrives. The marques leaves his wedding party early to spend the night with Martha. When he appears at the house of the newlyweds, a fight results. Pedro strangles the landowner as the villagers, who hate the despotic marques, look on. The final image shows Pedro and Martha as they head for the mountains together.

D Leni Riefenstahl; DG Georg Wilhelm Pabst, Arthur Maria Rabenalt; AD Harald Reinl; PC Riefenstahl-Film, Berlin (Tobis Filmkunst, Berlin) (until 1945), Plesner Film; P Leni Riefenstahl, Josef Plesner; EP Max Hüske, Walter Traut; C Albert Benitz; SP Rolf Lantin; E Leni Riefenstahl; SW Leni Riefenstahl, Harald Reinl; M The play "Terra baixa" (1896) by Angel Guimerà and the opera "Tiefland" (1903) by Eugen d'Albert; S Rudolf Kaiser, Herbert Janeczka; M Herbert Windt using melodies from d'Albert's opera; Sets Erich Grave, Isabella Ploberger; interior decor: Paul Prätel; exterior decor: Fritz Bollenhagen; Co Gustav Jäger, Elisabeth Massary; Ma Paul Lange, Franz Siebert
Dist Allianz Verleih, Deutsche Cosmopol, Taurus (video); SD 1940 to 1944; EL Krün in the Karwendel Mountains, the Rosengarten massif in the Dolomites, the area around Madrid; Stu UFA Studios Babelsberg, Barrandov Studios in Prague; Prem 11 February 1954 EM-Theater, Stuttgart
A Leni Riefenstahl, Franz Eichberger, Bernhard Minetti, Aribert Wäscher, Maria Koppenhöfer (Speaker: Til Klockow), Luis Rainer, Frida Richard, Karl Skraup, Max Holzboer, Bekuch Hamid, Charlotte Komp, Hans Lackner
Sound film, b/w, 8,840 feet, 99 minutes, 35 mm, 1:1.33

Notes Although work begins on the project in 1934, it is shelved by Terra, the production company, when the director becomes ill. In 1939 Tobis picks it up again, but the outbreak of the war, scheduling problems with the actors, difficulties building the village for the film, booking the studio, and especially finding a wolf cause repeated delays. After four years, in 1944, the film is finally completed. After the war the footage is confiscated by the French and not returned to the director until 1953. Because some of the material originally shot is missing or damaged, the film finished by Leni Riefenstahl does not include all of the scenes that were planned and shot.

UNREALIZED FILM PROJECTS
NICHT REALISIERTE FILMPROJEKTE

1933

Planned Title MADEMOISELLE DOCTEUR
Idea Arnold Fanck, Leni Riefenstahl **Direction** G. W. Pabst or Frank Wysbar **Production** UFA, Karl Ritter's production group **Script** Gerhard Menzel **Camera** Hans Schneeberger **Cast** Leni Riefenstahl
Subject The script tells the true story of a spy who works for German defense forces during World War I. The UFA initially accepts the film project but later turns it down because of the spy theme, following a request from the Ministry of Defense. In 1936 Georg Wilhelm Pabst directs "Mademoiselle Docteur" in France with Dita Parlo, using a different script.

1939

Planned Title PENTHESILEA
Idea/Script Leni Riefenstahl, based on a play by Heinrich von Kleist **Direction** Leni Riefenstahl, Jürgen Fehling **Production** Leni Riefenstahl-Film **Camera** Hans Schneeberger, Albert Benitz **Sets** Robert Herlth, Walter Röhrig **Music** Herbert Windt **Cast** Leni Riefenstahl, Maria Koppenhöfer, Elisabeth Flickenschildt, extras for the Amazons **Scheduled filming** Fall 1939 **Exterior Locations** Libyan desert and either the island of Sylt or the Kurisch Spit
Subject The dialogue would use Kleist's verse. The battle of the sexes is not planned as filmed theater; the lyrical language of Kleist and the stylized images are meant to form a unity.
The director prepares the filming, hires the actors and crew, finds mastiffs and Lipizzan horses for the film, and learns to ride bareback. With the outbreak of the war on 1 September 1939, however, filming is called off and for reasons of cost never resumed.

1943

Planned Title VAN GOGH
Idea Leni Riefenstahl
Subject A film about the artist's passion, his genius, and madness. Filming is to be primarily in black-and-white; only the scenes that depict the painting process are to be shot in color.
The project is not pursued.

1950

Planned Title THE DANCER OF FLORENCE
Idea Leni Riefenstahl
Subject A homage to the dancer Harald Kreutzberg.
No producer can be found for the idea.

1950

Planned Title ETERNAL PEAKS
Idea Leni Riefenstahl
Subject A documentary film about four historical first climbs of famous mountains throughout the world: Mont Blanc, the north face of the Drei Zinnen, the Eiger, and Mount Everest.
No producer can be found for the idea.

1950–1954

Planned Title THE RED DEVILS
Idea Leni Riefenstahl **Script** Leni Riefenstahl, Harald Reinl, Joachim Bartsch **Production** Capital Pictures (Italy); after Capital's withdrawal in 1952, Minerva Film (Italy) and Herzog-Film (Germany) coproduced with Iris-Film; from 1953 on, Junta-Film **Camera** Bruno Mondi, Walter Frentz, Guzzi Lantschner, Otto Lantschner **Cast** Vittorio De Sica, Brigitte Bardot, Jean Marais, male and female skiers
Subject The skiing film "The Red Devils" is a variation on the Penthesilea theme and is planned as a color film. The climax of the film is to be a "fox hunt" with skiers in red and blue outfits, making a sharp color contrast with the snow-covered slopes and mountains.
The film falls through for lack of financing.

1955

Planned Title COBALT 60
Idea Leni Riefenstahl
Subject A documentary and feature film on the destructive potential of nuclear power.
No producer can be found for the idea.

Krater.

Registering the title for the film "Penthesilea" at the Reich film board, March 1939.

Vincent van Gogh, self-portrait, 1889.

Harald Kreutzberg.

1955

Planned Title FREDERICK THE GREAT AND VOLTAIRE
Idea Jean Cocteau **Script** Leni Riefenstahl, Herrmann Mostar **Cast** Jean Cocteau
Subject A black-and-white film intended to thematize the relationship of the king and the philosopher – and the love-hate relationship of the Germans and French. Jean Cocteau plans to play both roles.
No producer can be found for the idea.

1955

Planned Title THREE STARS ON THE CLOAK OF THE MADONNA
Idea Leni Riefenstahl **Script** Leni Riefenstahl, Margarete E. Hohoff **Cast** Anna Magnani
Subject A woman loses her husband and three sons. She endures her fate thanks to the strength of her faith.
No producer can be found for the idea.

1955

Planned Title THE BULL FIGHT OF MONSIEUR CHATALON/DANCE WITH DEATH
Idea/Script Leni Riefenstahl, Herrmann Mostar **Production** Cea (Spain)
Subject Stories concerning bullfighting in Spain.
No producer can be found for the idea.

1955

Planned Title SOL Y SOMBRA (SUN AND SHADOW)
Idea/Script Leni Riefenstahl **Production** Cea (Spain)
Subject Documentary film on the religious, geographic and architectural variety of Spain.
Cea withdraws from the project.

1955–1956

Planned Title BLACK FREIGHT
Idea Leni Riefenstahl, based on a work by Hans Otto Meissner **Script** Leni Riefenstahl, Helge Pawlinin, Kurt Heuser **Direction** Leni Riefenstahl **Production** Stern-Film with Lawrence-Brown Safaris, Nairobi **Camera** Heinz Hölschner, R. von Theumer **Cast** Leni Riefenstahl, extras from the Jalau tribe, Arab extras **Sched-**uled filming Early September to late November 1956 **Exterior Locations** Kenya, Queen Elizabeth National Park in Uganda
Subject A scientist is searching for her lost husband in Africa and becomes caught up in the modern slave trade.
The Suez crisis delays the shooting because the ship carrying the equipment has to round the cape, resulting in several weeks' delay. For financial reasons the project is halted and cannot be continued as no backers can be found.

1957

Planned Title AFRICAN SYMPHONY
Idea Leni Riefenstahl **Script** Leni Riefenstahl, Helge Pawlinin
Subject A look at Africa from four different perspectives: from the realistic perspective of a reporter, the surrealistic-romantic view of an artist, the adventurous tale of a hunter and the ethnological enquiry of the scientist.
No producer can be found for the idea.

1959–1960

Planned Title THE BLUE LIGHT
Script initially W. Somerset Maugham; from 1960 on L. Ron Hubbard, Philip Hudsmith based on the original script by Leni Riefenstahl and Béla Balázs **Direction** Leni Riefenstahl **Production** Adventure Film Ltd., London
The remake of "The Blue Light" is planned as a dance film in color, in the style of "The Red Shoes" (1948). The new 70-mm wide-screen technique is to be used in this film.
Adventure Film withdraws from the project.

1961

Planned Title THE NILE
Direction Leni Riefenstahl **Production** Kondo-Film
Subject Together with her partners in the Kondo-Film company – the Berlin-based Japanese film enthusiasts Michi, Yoshi, and Yasu Kondo – she plans a documentary that will depict the life and customs of the various native peoples on the banks of the Nile. With the building of the Berlin Wall on 13 August 1961, the Kondo brothers return to Tokyo, Kondo-Film is dissolved, and the film project falls through.

1962–1963

Planned Title AFRICAN DIARY
Direction Leni Riefenstahl
She plans a small documentary film, to be made during a scientific expedition led by the German Nansen Society to the Nuer tribe in the southern Sudan. She takes part in the expedition to the Nuba village of Tadoro, but later the Nansen Society leaves her, and she travels on alone.

1964–1975

Planned Title ALONE AMONG THE NUBA
Idea Leni Riefenstahl **Production** Odyssey Productions (USA) and Leni Riefenstahl-Film **Camera** Gerhard Fromm, from 1968 on Horst Kettner and Leni Riefenstahl
Subject Documentary film on the life of the Nuba. During the winter of 1964–1965 in Tadoro, Leni Riefenstahl films the wrestling matches, ritual acts, dances, and daily life of the Nuba.
The new, highly light-sensitive ER film is destroyed in processing. Odyssey Productions then withdraws from the project, which is put off for the time being. During later expeditions in 1968–1969, 1974, and 1975, she films again in the Nuba villages of Tadoro and Kau but never completes the final edit.

1976–PRESENT

Planned Title UNDERWATER FILM
Idea Leni Riefenstahl **Camera** Horst Kettner, Leni Riefenstahl **Production** Riefenstahl-Produktion GmbH
Subject Film about the undersea world.
She films with Horst Kettner in various diving regions throughout the world. Excerpts from the footage can be seen in Ray Müller's documentary "The Wonderful, Horrible Life of Leni Riefenstahl" (1993).

The script of "The Red Devils."   Jean Cocteau (right).   "Black Freight", 1955–1956.

BIOGRAPHY
LENI RIEFENSTAHL

1902

Helene Amalia Bertha Riefenstahl is born on 22 August in the Wedding district of Berlin. Her father, Alfred Theodor Paul Riefenstahl (1878–1944), descended from a family of craftsmen in Brandenburg, establishes a successful firm that installs modern heating, ventilation and sanitary equipment in new buildings in Berlin. Built-in plumbing and central heating are among the newest technical achievements in home construction and are thus a lucrative field. Leni Riefenstahl describes her father as a forward-thinking businessman who was always interested in technological innovations but who was also hot-tempered and domineering. Her mother, Bertha Ida Riefenstahl, née Scherlach (1880–1965), was the 18th child of a master builder from West Prussia. Both parents love the theater and attend performances frequently. When her husband goes hunting at weekends, Bertha Riefenstahl secretly attends balls or goes to the cinema with her daughter.

1905

Her brother, Heinz, is born. The two siblings share a very close relationship.

1914–1917

In 1914 she becomes a member of the Nixe swimming club and also joins a gymnastics club without her father's permission. After a serious accident, her father forbids her to continue gymnastics and instead she learns roller- and ice-skating. She also likes to read fairy tales and to write short poems. Her father wants Heinz to follow him into the family business, while his daughter is to go to school in home economics. But the children have their own dreams: Heinz wants to be an architect and Leni an actress.

1918

She successfully completes her schooling at the Kollmorgen Lyceum in Berlin. In early

Previous page: Leni as a two-year-old. Below: As a young woman, her mother dreamed of becoming an actress.

Bertha Scherlach and Alfred Riefenstahl marry on 5 April 1902. Almost five months later Leni is born.

The Riefenstahl family at a large family gathering, around 1910. Leni is sitting in front at the left; her younger brother, Heinz, is standing in front on the right; their parents are in the center of the back row.

During a swimming excursion at Lake Zeuthen near Berlin, circa 1912, where the family often spent the weekend. With great enthusiasm Leni learns to swim and joins the Nixe swimming club in 1914.

summer she sees a newspaper advertisement seeking young actresses for the film *Opium* (1919); she attends the audition at the Helene Grimm-Reiter Dance School on Berlin's Kurfürstendamm. She is so taken by its atmosphere that, without her father's permission but with the support of her mother, she secretly attends courses in expressive dance and classical ballet. The Grimm-Reiter School is also where Anita Berber is rehearsing, who as a nude dancer in the 1920s would help to define the expressive dance style in Berlin with provocative *Dances of Horror, Vice, and Ecstasy*. When Anita Berber is unable to fulfill a scheduled dance performance, Leni Riefenstahl spontaneously agrees to dance in her place. Her first performance is a success, but now Alfred Riefenstahl learns of her dance lessons. He considers dance disreputable, and he forbids her to continue. In keeping with his wishes, in the autumn she attends the State School for Arts and Crafts for a semester to study painting.

1919

Her father nevertheless sends her to a boarding school in Thale in the Harz Mountains for a year. There she secretly practices dance, performs drama with the other girls, directs, and visits performances at the open-air theater in Thale.

1920

Father and daughter reach a compromise: If Leni will work as a secretary in his business, her father will permit her to take dance lessons at the Grimm-Reiter School and perform in public. Meanwhile the family is now living outside Berlin, in Zeuthen. In her free time Leni learns to play tennis.

1921–1922

Following a second dispute with her father, she moves out of her parents' home briefly. Finally, Alfred Riefenstahl resigns himself to

Later her parents purchase property on the banks of Lake Zeuthen. There Leni writes her first poems and plays.

Leni as a four-year-old.

Leni's school class (she is on the far right in the first row) at the Kollmorgen Lyceum in Berlin, around 1914.

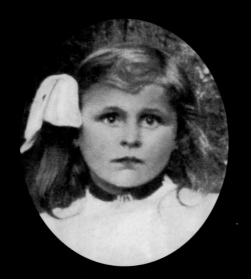

his daughter's dreams of the stage, and she begins training in classical ballet under Eugenie Eduardova, a former ballerina from St. Petersburg. In the afternoon she also takes lessons in expressive dance at the Jutta Klamt School. Her dance education lasts just two years in all, but she practices so intensively that she catches up with the other students who began at a younger age. During a vacation on the Baltic Sea she meets Harry (Henry) R. Sokal, a young businessman from Innsbruck who will later lend financial support to her first dance performances and her first independent film production.

1923

For half a year she attends the Dresden dance school of the famous Mary Wigman, a founder of modern expressive dance. There Leni Riefenstahl dances together with fellow students Gret Palucca, Yvonne Georgi, and Vera Skoronell. She choreographs on her own the cycle *The Three Dances of Eros*, to music by Tchaikovsky, Chopin and Grieg, which will later become part of her stage program. Back in Berlin, she continues her dance education with Jutta Klamt and Eugenie Eduardova. In a salon she meets the Italian pianist and composer Ferruccio Busoni, who composes a waltz for her. She choreographs more dances, including her personal favorite, *The Unfinished,* to music by Schubert, and *Dance to the Sea,* to music by Beethoven. On 23 October she has her first solo performance, with dances she has choreographed herself, at the Tonhalle in Munich. The evening is financed by Harry Sokal and is a great success – as is her solo recital several days later at the Blüthner Hall in Berlin. Max Reinhardt, a founder of modern theater directing, engages her for several solo performances in his world-famous Deutsches Theater and in his Kammerspiele in Berlin. She is accoladed in Frankfurt, Leipzig, Düsseldorf, Cologne, Dresden, Kiel, Stettin, in the Schau-

spielhaus in Zürich and the Central Concert House in Prague. She participates in more than 70 dance performances, most of which comprise about 15 dances she has choreographed herself. The background of the stage is kept black to emphasize the dance and the effective use of lighting. Bertha Riefenstahl always accompanies her daughter and sews the costumes Leni Riefenstahl designs herself. No longer a minor and now financially independent, the dancer moves into her first apartment in Fasanenstrasse, in the Wilmersdorf district of Berlin, near the Kurfürstendamm.

1924

Injures her knee in a dance performance in Prague and is forced to stop dancing for a time. Becomes engaged to Otto Froitzheim, the internationally successful German tennis champion. A turning point in her life comes with *Mountain of Destiny* (1924), a mountain film set in the Dolomites by Arnold Fanck. On the way to a doctor's appointment, she happens to see the film poster and is so fascinated that she misses the appointment and instead sees the film over and over again. Some weeks later, she even travels to the Dolomites to meet the lead actor, Luis Trenker, in person. Later, in Berlin, Leni Riefenstahl meets Arnold Fanck, the most important director of mountain films, a genre of German film that depicts the protagonists set in landscapes of snow and cliffs at high altitudes, where they are subjected to the forces of elements. In contrast to other directors, Fanck, originally a documentary filmmaker, films on location in the Alps, not in the studio. He founds the so-called Freiburg School, a team of outstanding mountain climbers and skiers who serve as cameramen but also as actors, extras, and stuntmen. In doing so, Fanck is breaking with the division of labor that is still common in production of feature films. Films like *Das Wunder des Schnee-*

Facing page: With her brother, Heinz, around 1912. The two siblings share a very close relationship.
Photo: Studio M. Appel

Leni and a friend, 1918, during a dance performance at their ballet school.

At the age of 18. Now her father permits her to take ballet lessons with Eugenie Eduardova, a Russian prima ballerina from St. Petersburg.

Portrait, around 1920.

Program for her solo performance at the Prague Central Concert House on 27 November 1923. She performs dances she has choreographed herself.

Portrait as a 15-year-old student. Leni dreams of becoming an actress, but her father forbids this aspiration.

schuhs (The Miracle of the Snowshoe, 1919–1920), *Im Kampf mit den Bergen* (The Fight with the Mountain, 1921) or *Fuchsjagd auf Skiern durchs Engadin* (The Fox Hunt on Skis in Engadine, 1920–1921) are convincing in their artistically and technically accomplished depictions of natural phenomena and breakneck athletic action scenes. Leni Riefenstahl has to undergo an extensive operation on her injured knee. She spends three months in hospital, and during this time Arnold Fanck is writing the script for the film *The Holy Mountain,* in which she is to play the dancer Diotima. She takes the lead with an eye to continuing her dance career later. She breaks off her engagement to Otto Froitzheim following an argument.

1925

In January filming for *The Holy Mountain* begins in the Grisons. The male leads are taken by Luis Trenker and Fanck's nephew Ernst Petersen. Bad weather, storms, and injuries drag out the filming longer and longer, until finally a second winter has to be worked into the schedule. This is Arnold Fanck's first film for UFA. From now on, Leni Riefenstahl belongs to Arnold Fanck's regular crew, as its only woman. The group gives her skiing instructions for this first film role and later teaches her mountain climbing as well, which she soon masters perfectly. During the filming she becomes enthusiastic for the craft of filmmaking. She learns how to create lighting effects, is soon able to work with different lenses, discovers the importance of different color filters and focal lengths, learns how film is developed and printed. For the first time she directs a few minor shots like the spring scene in the Bernese Oberland and later the torch-lit shots in St. Anton on the Arlberg. She is especially interested in editing as a creative process. In the circle around Fanck she learns how important teamwork is in film production and later as a director she will

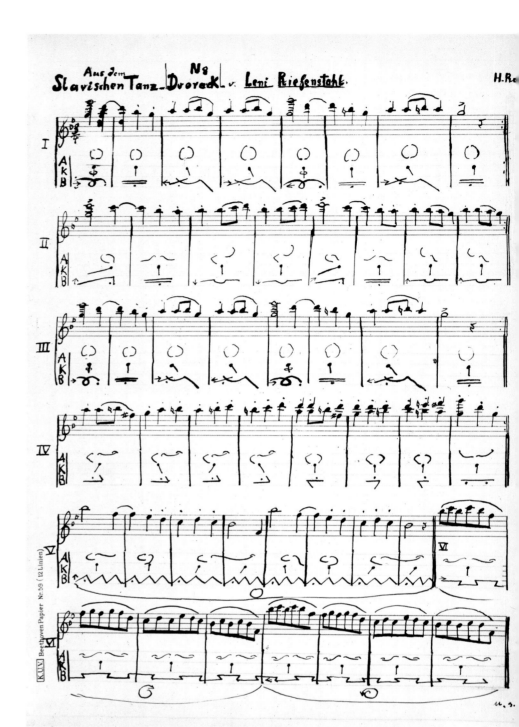

Program for the dance performance at the Public Theater of Grünberg in Silesia on 8 April 1924.

She performs a solo dance at the Public Theater of Chemnitz on 11 June 1924.

Her dance "Valse Caprice", to music by Ferruccio Busoni, is a great success.
Photo: Karl Schenker

She becomes engaged to the successful German tennis champion Otto Froitzheim in 1924.
Photo: Binder

Her successful dance "Summer" to music by Antonín Dvořák.
Photo: Studio Schenker

engage the same set of coworkers as much as possible, frequently including members of the Freiburg School.

1926

In January the filming for *The Holy Mountain* is continued on the Feldberg and the Arlberg. Leni Riefenstahl has to be trapped under an avalanche in front of the camera, because Arnold Fanck insists on the authenticity of all the shots and does not permit doubles or studio shots. For the final wedding scene Fanck builds the "Ice Cathedral," a 50-foot-high hall of ice made of stalactites, on a frozen lake in Lenzerheide in the Grisons. Even as the filming continues, Leni Riefenstahl resumes her dance training and reworks her choreography to use in the dance scenes of the film. For the dance scene at the seashore, to music by Beethoven, she synchronizes her movements to the surf and breakers. She begins to accept dance performances again, appearing on stage in Düsseldorf, Frankfurt, Berlin, Dresden, Leipzig, Kassel, and Cologne. Her last official dance performance takes place on the stage of the cinema for the premiere of *The Holy Mountain* at the UFA-Palast am Zoo in Berlin.

1927

She is offered and accepts the lead in Arnold Fanck's next film and thus decides once and for all to give up dancing in favor of an acting career. The two years spent filming create a gap in her dance training, and at 24 she feels too old for dancing. Her costars in the comedy *The Great Leap* are Hans Schneeberger, a brilliant ski racer and member of the Freiburg School, and Luis Trenker, who will soon leave Arnold Fanck to make his own successful mountain films, including *Mountains in Flames* (1931) and *The Rebel* (1932). The shooting takes place on the Arlberg and in the Dolomites under conditions that are physically demanding for the actors.

Leni Riefenstahl choreographs all her dances herself. Her manuscript notes on the choreography of the "Slavonic Dances" to music by Antonín Dvořák reveal how precisely the dancer has coordinated her movements with the music.

AAFA publicity still of Dr. Arnold Fanck, circa 1930. The founder of the genre of the mountain film casts her in 6 leading roles. Photo: Etzieber

Publicity still of the famous French director Abel Gance, friend and admirer of Leni Riefenstahl, with a dedication dated 10 October 1928.

On an excursion in 1926 with the dream couple of German film, Willy Fritsch and Lilian Harvey (right), and the actresses Camilla Horn (above) and Christa Tordy (below). Photo: Neue Illustrierte

For her second leading role, Leni Riefenstahl has to learn even barefoot rock climbing and to swim in Lake Carezza in water at 43°F; the actors often stand around for hours in ice-cold glacier streams; and Hans Schneeberger takes acrobatic falls wearing a rubber suit that is filled with air. After the shooting, Leni Riefenstahl moves with Hans Schneeberger into a three-room apartment with a dance studio in the Wilmersdorf district of Berlin, where they live together for several years.

1928

In February she travels to St. Moritz with Arnold Fanck and Hans Schneeberger, who film the Winter Olympic Games there. She describes her impressions in her first article, which is published in *Film-Kurier*. Since then she regularly publishes reports in various film journals about the filming of her works and she often writes her own publicity releases. In the film center of Berlin she seeks out roles that will take her beyond the genre of the mountain film, because working as an actress under Fanck is unsatisfying from a dramatic standpoint. In the now-lost film *The Destiny of the Hapsburgs,* under the direction of Rolf Raffé, she plays the Baroness Mary Vetsera, the lover of Rudolf, heir to the throne at the Vienna court. The shooting takes place in Schönbrunn Palace in Vienna, where she plays alongside the famous actresses Erna Morena and Maly Delschaft. In Berlin she makes friends with the famous French film director Abel Gance, who has made a mark in film history by introducing a new wide-screen technique, unusual processes for dissolving between images, double exposures, and a mobile camera in his film *Napoléon* (1927). She becomes acquainted with the director Walther Ruttmann, who garners attention for his experimental documentary *Berlin: Symphony of a Great City* (1927), and the famous director Georg Wilhelm Pabst.

Her next engagement is the leading role in another mountain film by Arnold Fanck: *The White Hell of Pitz Palu,* which is filmed in the Engadine Valley on the Morteratsch Glacier and at Pitz Palu, where the whole film crew lives in cramped quarters in the Diavolezza shelter. The filming takes more than six months in all. Leni Riefenstahl's partners are Ernst Petersen and Gustav Diessl, a famous actor in the adventure films of the 1920s and 1930s. Diessl will later act in *The Tiger of Eshnapur* (1938) by Richard Eichberg. For the first time the famous stunt pilot Ernst Udet, with whom she remains friends until his suicide in 1941, takes the role of a rescue pilot. Temperatures of minus 18°F create very difficult conditions for the actors and cameramen, but they nevertheless obtain fantastic images of the snow-covered mountains. Fanck has high cliff faces sprayed with water so that they ice over, and then used propellers to simulate a snowstorm. Leni Riefenstahl is pulled up an ice face on a rope while an avalanche descends on her from above. In another scene she stands in for her colleague Mizzi Götzel, who, as the script specifies, falls backward into a glacier crevasse 50 feet deep. Innovative shooting techniques make for impressive images: mountain guides and cameramen with magnesium torches rappel into crevasses as deep as 150 feet at night in order to film the reflections of the torchlight on the walls of ice. Codirector Georg Wilhelm Pabst works with the actors. Arnold Fanck lets the actors improvise, whereas Pabst directs them very precisely and helps them to identify with their respective roles. In *The White Hell of Pitz Palu* Leni Riefenstahl gives her best acting performance under someone else's direction. At the end of the filming Hans Schneeberger breaks up with her. In Berlin she meets the Austrian-American director Josef von Sternberg, who is filming *The Blue Angel* (1929–1930) in Babels-

With Marlene Dietrich and the Hollywood star Anna May Wong at a Berlin ball in 1928. Each of the three actresses embodies a different type of woman: Leni Riefenstahl is the epitome of the modern, athletic woman, whereas Marlene Dietrich is depicted by Josef von Sternberg as a vamp, and Anna May Wong conquers the screen as an exotic beauty.
© Alfred Eisenstaedt/ TimePix/inter Topics

Leni Riefenstahl and the director Georg Wilhelm Pabst are two of the stars of the Berlin Film Ball of 1930. Pabst's wife, Gertrude, is on the left.

With (from left to right) Arnold Fanck, the stunt pilot Ernst Udet, and the producer Paul Kohner during the preparations for "SOS Iceberg", 1932.

berg with Marlene Dietrich, and Emil Jannings. She rejects Sternberg's offer to accompany him back to Hollywood.

1930

She accepts another leading role under Arnold Fanck's direction: *Storm over Mont Blanc* is the first sound film for both her and Fanck, though dialogue and sound effects are added later in the studio. With the sound technique of the time, in which dialogue, the sounds on the set, and the music are recorded simultaneously with the images on a light-sensitive track, sound recordings are impossible in the mountains. For the male lead she suggests the amateur actor Sepp Rist, who is working as a police radio operator in Nuremberg and is an excellent skier. Without Fanck's knowledge, she has Sepp Rist come for a screen test, and the director does indeed hire him. He will later perform in several other mountain films, including *Geierwally* (1940) by Hans Steinhoff. During filming the entire crew spends several weeks at the Vallot shelter on Mont Blanc, and again storms, avalanches, and cracks in the glaciers are daily occurrences on the set. In one scene Leni Riefenstahl has to cross a rickety ladder over a 150-foot-deep crevasse in the Bosson Glacier, and later she is in the cockpit when Ernst Udet makes the first landing ever on a glacier, the Mont Blanc Glacier. Back in Berlin she trains her voice for sound films and takes speech lessons. She writes film treatments and the manuscript for what will become her own first film, *The Blue Light*. In contrast to Arnold Fanck, who associates realistic and athletic themes with the expressive landscape of the mountains, Leni Riefenstahl seeks a romantic and mystic subject for her film and sets it in an artistic Alpine landscape. To raise start-up costs for the film, she sells personal possessions and earns money as the lead in Arnold Fanck's ski comedy *The White Flame*.

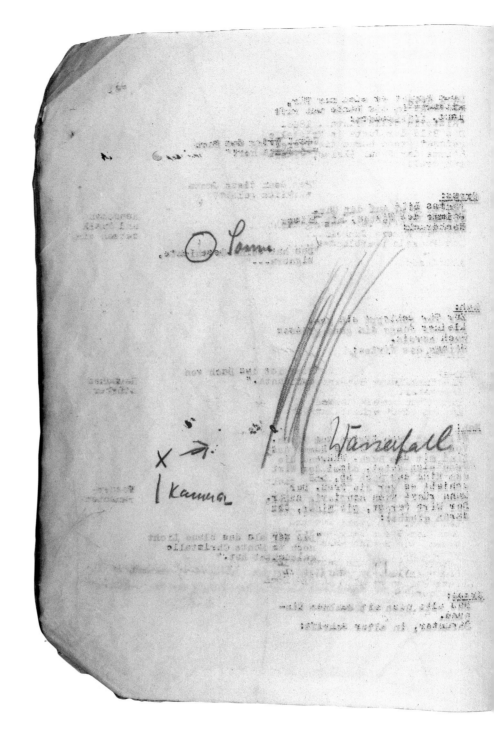

The director at the camera during the filming of "The Blue Light" on the Rosengarten massif in the Dolomites, summer 1931.

Leni Riefenstahl demonstrates to her cameraman the shot she wants on Crozzon in the Dolomites, summer 1931.

One of the farmers from the Sarn Valley who, after completing the annual harvest, play villagers in "The Blue Light".

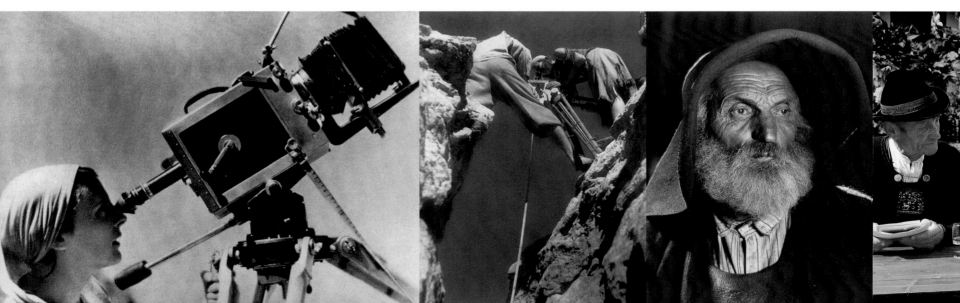

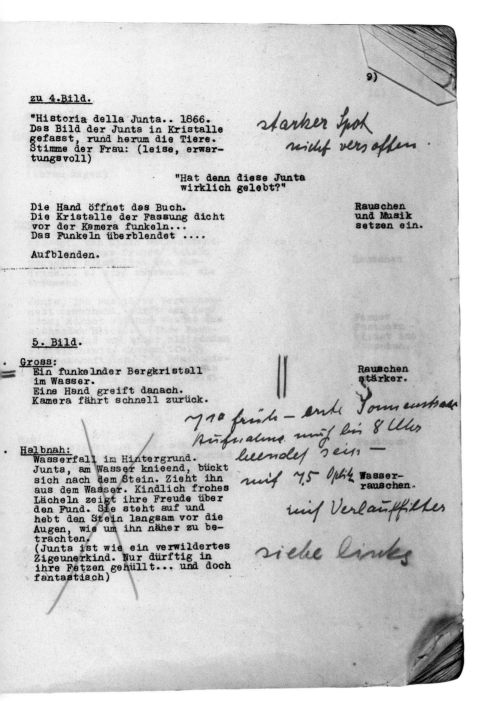

zu 4.Bild.

"Historia della Junta.. 1866.
Das Bild der Junta in Kristalle
gefasst, rund herum die Tiere.
Stimme der Frau: (leise, erwar-
tungsvoll)

          "Hat denn diese Junta
           wirklich gelebt?"

Die Hand öffnet das Buch.
Die Kristalle der Fassung dicht
vor der Kamera funkeln...
Das Funkeln überblendet ....

Aufblenden.

5. Bild.

Gross:
Ein funkelnder Bergkristall
im Wasser.
Eine Hand greift danach.
Kamera fährt schnell zurück.

Halbnah:
Wasserfall im Hintergrund.
Junta, am Wasser kniend, bückt
sich nach dem Stein. Zieht ihn
aus dem Wasser. Kindlich frohes
Lächeln zeigt ihre Freude über
den Fund. Sie steht auf und
hebt den Stein langsam vor die
Augen, wie um ihn näher zu betrachten.
(Junta ist wie ein verwildertes
Zigeunerkind. Nur dürftig in
ihre Fetzen gehüllt... und doch
fantastisch)

A page from the script of "The Blue Light" showing the director's handwritten notes on the position of the sun and the resulting schedule for the filming. The camera position and possible lenses are also precisely noted.

1931

She spends five months in St. Anton and Zürs on the Arlberg for the shooting of *The White Flame*. The best skiers of the time, including Hannes Schneider and Rudi Matt, play roles in the film. At the same time she continues work on her own project *The Blue Light*. She gets Béla Balázs, the famous German-Hungarian film theorist and screenwriter, to collaborate on the script. A communist, he leaves for the Soviet Union in the autumn of 1931; after his emigration he lives in Moscow and later in Budapest. During the Third Reich, because of his Jewish origins, his name will be removed from the film's credits, but until his death in 1949 he will remain friends with Leni Riefenstahl. For the project Béla Balázs also takes control of Leni Riefenstahl's scenes. Each scene is marked with the precise camera position, the possible lenses, and the ideal focal length. Leni Riefenstahl immediately invests her earnings from *The White Flame* in the production of *The Blue Light*. She establishes her first film company, with herself as the sole owner: Leni Riefenstahl Studio-Film. After the first test shots, the firm Henry R. Sokal-Produktion, which has already coproduced three of Arnold Fanck's mountain films, takes on coproduction. *The Blue Light* can be produced only because Leni Riefenstahl keeps the crew to a minimum. She directs and edits the film herself in addition to producing it and taking the lead. Most of the small crew either agree to defer their pay until the film is released or even work without pay altogether. She also films on location in the Alps, thereby avoiding expensive studio shots. *The Blue Light* can thus be considered an early auteur film. She selects her crew from past films with Arnold Fanck: the cameraman Hans Schneeberger, the actors Beni Führer, Max Holzboer as well as the set builder Leopold Blonder. In June she starts to seek out locations and actors. The village Foroglio, next to a waterfall in the

Among the farmers in the Sarn Valley, around 1990. Whenever Leni Riefenstahl is in Bolzano, she visits "her" farmers.

"The Blue Light" is enthusiastically received and later runs for weeks in sold-out theaters in both France and England. Here is the premiere of the film in Düsseldorf.

Enthusiastic spectators wait for the director at the premiere of "The Blue Light".

Maggia Valley in Ticino and two hours by foot from the next village, suits her idea of the fictive Alpine village of Santa Maria; for the mountain shots she chooses Crozzon in the Brenta group of the Dolomites. After a long search, she locates mountain villagers in the Sarn Valley near Bolzano who have never left their valley and thus exude authenticity. Although they live in complete isolation on their mountain farms, they agree to play the role of villagers once they have finished the harvest. The director will remain in contact with these villagers for many years, and later she will hire a number of people from the Sarn Valley as extras for *Tiefland*. The shooting takes place from July to September. With great care the small crew tries out various camera angles. Every afternoon two crew members descend into the valley and have the shots from the most important scenes developed. The rushes are then compared the same evening to see whether the camera positions can be improved. The cameraman Hans Schneeberger works with the specially developed "R-Material" film stock, which, when used in conjunction with special color filters, makes day shots look like night ones, so that the dangerous climbing scenes can be filmed during daylight. In addition, Leni Riefenstahl and Hans Schneeberger experiment with various color filters and lenses to produce a fairytale-like atmosphere. For the interior shots they work on location, in farmhouses and a church, as well as with a lighting dolly, which is still quite unusual for the time. Later, in Berlin in a small studio, two days are spent shooting the scenes for the crystal grotto, which is constructed from polished glass shards. She edits the film herself, but she is unhappy with the result. She turns to Arnold Fanck, who re-edits her film, but almost destroys it in the process. Leni Riefenstahl begins editing again alone and completely rearranges the scenes, this time finding a rhythm of images that suits the fairytale

theme. The music is composed by the director of UFA's music department, Giuseppe Becce.

1932

The film *The Blue Light* has its premiere on 24 March 1932 in the UFA-Palast am Zoo in Berlin. It becomes a worldwide success and brings Leni Riefenstahl international fame as a producer, director, creator of images, and lead actress. At the Venice Film Biennale, which takes place for the first time, *The Blue Light* wins the silver medal. In February she hears a speech by Adolf Hitler in the Sports Palace in Berlin and is so impressed by his charisma that she writes him a letter in May, and he invites her to Horumersiel near Wilhelmshaven on the North Sea. Then she accepts her final starring role in a film by Arnold Fanck: in the German-American co-production *SOS Iceberg,* which takes place in Greenland. English and German versions are produced simultaneously, and Arnold Fanck shares a director's credit with the Hollywood director Tay Garnett for the slightly modified American version. Leni Riefenstahl plays the female lead in both versions; her costars in the German version are Gustav Diessl and Sepp Rist. Ernst Udet, with three airplanes, takes part once again. In late May the whole crew – including two polar bears from Hamburg Zoo – travel to Greenland for five months with a special permit from the Danish government. At the time, only scientific expeditions are granted permission from the Danish government to travel to Greenland. For that reason, the crew is accompanied by the Danish polar explorer Knud Rasmussen and two German researchers who took part in the Alfred Wegener expedition of 1931 and who now act as scientific advisors to the film crew. The expedition has 37 members in all, including nine women. For five months the film crew lives in a tent camp near the Eskimo village of Umanak, on the northwest

With Hitler, discussing the preparations for the Sixth Party Rally of 1934 in Nuremberg. She tries unsuccessfully to convince him to have another director make the film.

During the winter 1934–1935 she works intensely for five months on the editing of "Triumph of the Will".

For the premiere of "Triumph of the Will" on 28 March 1935, Albert Speer decorates the lobby of the Berlin UFA-Palast am Zoo.

"Newsweek" dedicates its 15 September 1934 cover to Leni Riefenstahl.

coast. The film's story of a lost polar explorer repeats itself on the set, when one of the scientists, Dr. Ernst Sorge, does not return from an excursion and can only be found with the help of Udet and his plane. As the primary director, Arnold Fanck films a glacier that is breaking up and tries out scenes on icebergs and ice floes – experiments which are extremely dangerous for the crew, because the icebergs can break off or spin around unexpectedly at any moment. During filming Knud Rasmussen keeps the crew informed about the speed of the moving icebergs, which can cover distances as great as 60 miles within a few hours. For several scenes the actors have to swim in ice-cold water, and Sepp Rist develops a serious case of rheumatism. Leni Riefenstahl is forced to leave the set early, because her bladder colic becomes unbearable. In late September she is back in Berlin, where she meets with Adolf Hitler again. Her friend Manfred George – editor of the Berlin evening newspaper *Tempo* and from 1939 on publisher of *Aufbau,* a German-language Jewish newspaper published in New York – asks her to write a series of articles about her experiences in Greenland. These result in 1933 in the book *Kampf in Schnee und Eis* (literally: Struggle in Snow and Ice), which depicts the strenuous and dangerous work of shooting mountain films.

1933

The final shooting for *SOS Iceberg* takes place over several months in the Bernina Pass, where an arctic landscape with enormous ice caves is constructed for the scenes. When she returns to Berlin in June, many of her Jewish acquaintances and friends have already emigrated: Manfred George, Max Reinhardt, UFA film producer Erich Pommer, stage star Elisabeth Bergner, and even Harry Sokal. Leni Riefenstahl is stunned and in despair. When, several days later, she receives

an invitation from the Reich chancellery, she speaks to Hitler about the emigration of her friends. Leni Riefenstahl describes this speech in her memoirs (p. 137) as follows: "Hitler raised his hand as if to stem my flow of words. Rather angrily he said, 'Fräulein Riefenstahl, I know how you feel; you told me as much in Horumersiel. I respect you. But I would like to ask you not to talk to me about a topic that I find disagreeable. I have great esteem for you as an artist, you have a rare talent, and I do not wish to influence you. But I cannot discuss the Jewish problem with you.'" After the success of *The Blue Light,* Leni Riefenstahl hopes to play dramatic roles in the future. The UFA contracts her for *Mademoiselle Docteur,* a project about a spy in World War I; she is to play the lead role under the famous director Frank Wysbar, and the dramaturge is Gerhard Menzel. But the Ministry of Defense forbids the project because no more spy films are to be produced in Germany. A few days before the National Socialist party rally in Nuremberg, she is called to the Reich chancellery, where Hitler asks her how far her preparations for the party rally film have progressed. Several months earlier, via his adjutant Wilhelm Brückner, he had told Joseph Goebbels and the Propaganda Ministry to give her this assignment; until this visit to Hitler, however, she had heard nothing about it. Leni Riefenstahl describes the conversation with Hitler at the Reich chancellery in her memoirs (p. 143): "'Why wasn't Fräulein Riefenstahl informed?' As he spoke he clenched his fists, glaring with anger. Before his terrified aide could reply, Hitler jeered, 'I can imagine how the gentlemen at the Propaganda Ministry must envy this gifted young artist. They can't stand the fact that such an honour has been awarded to a woman – and, indeed, an artist who isn't even a member of the Party.'" A heated discussion between Hitler and Goebbels follows, and this merely reinforces

In 1936 "Time" also publishes a title story on the director.

The certificate for the gold medal that Leni Riefenstahl is awarded for "Triumph of the Will" at the World Fair in Paris in 1937.

In front of her house, summer 1937. At the front: Adolf Hitler; Leni Riefenstahl; Joseph Goebbels; Dr. Ebersberg; Leni's sister-in-law, Ilse; back row: her brother, Heinz, and her mother. This photograph is taken for the international press after a Swiss magazine claims that Leni Riefenstahl has been forced to leave Germany because of her Jewish ancestry. Photo: Heinrich Hoffmann

Goebbel's dislike of Leni Riefenstahl and is one of the causes behind the quarrels that the director will have with him and the Propaganda Ministry from then until the end of the war. Hitler insists that she travel to Nuremberg, despite the short notice and lack of preparation, in order to start filming. Without contract or funding, she travels to Nuremberg together with Sepp Allgeier, Franz Weihmayr, and the amateur cameraman Walter Frentz. Instead of receiving help from the party, however, she and her camera crew are completely boycotted. They are not even given film stock, so that she cannot begin shooting. She wants to leave, but then the architect Albert Speer meets her, and it is thanks to his influence that she is at least able to film some of the events. When the party rally ends, Hitler calls her back to the Reich chancellery to get a report on the filming. Leni Riefenstahl describes this encounter in her memoirs (p. 147): "Hitler's face turned crimson, while Goebbels became chalky white as the Führer leaped up and snapped: 'Doctor, you are responsible for this. It is not to happen again. The motion picture about the national Party rally [of 1934] is to be made by Fräulein Riefenstahl and not by the Party film people. Those are my orders!' Full of despair, I exclaimed: 'I can't, I absolutely can't!' Hitler's voice became icy. 'You can and you will. I apologize for what you have been through. It will not happen again'" The total production costs for the film *Victory of Faith* come to 60,000 reichsmarks, including the director's fee of 20,000 reichsmarks. Although she does not like the film, produced with such modest means, it is highly praised by the press and the party.

1934

Despite Hitler's order for her to film the party rally in 1934, Leni Riefenstahl still hopes to withdraw from the assignment. She asks her friend Walther Ruttmann, who was then the best documentary filmmaker, and whose film *Berlin: Symphony of a Great City* (1927) won prizes and has since become a classic, to direct the party rally film. Walther Ruttmann gladly accepts the assignment. Leni Riefenstahl is convinced that Walther Ruttmann will do a much better job than she could herself. She accepts an offer from the Berlin production company Terra-Film to direct and star in the film *Tiefland*. It is based on the renowned opera by Eugen d'Albert: a famous Catalan play that depicts the contrast between the traditional mountain world and the lowlands with their avaricious inhabitants. By accepting the film, Leni Riefenstahl hopes to escape Hitler's assignment. She dives into her work in Spain, playing the role of the Gypsy dancer Martha, with such great fervor that she suffers a breakdown and spends two months in a hospital in Madrid. The work on *Tiefland* has to be called off. Walther Ruttmann visits her in Spain several times to report on his work. When she returns to Berlin after her recovery and sees Walther Ruttmann's edit, she is incredulous, because the film is unbelievably bad. As she describes it in her memoirs, he could not visualize the effect that shots of the arena would have, and wanted to compensate by adding a plot. He wanted to depict in film how a party with just seven members could become a large popular party in just a few years. Because there was no footage of this history, however, he tried to present it through shots of posters, newspapers, documents, and weeklies. The attempt failed entirely, and Leni Riefenstahl realizes she cannot take responsibility for Ruttmann's film. Hitler would not accept it, and she will now have to make the film herself. Nevertheless, she makes one last desperate attempt to discuss it with Hitler, and she travels to Nuremberg to meet him. The dramatic dialogue there is described in Leni Riefenstahl's memoirs (pp. 157–58) as follows: "After our exchange of greetings he

Her house at Heydenstrasse 30 in the Dahlem district of Berlin, near Grunewald. In 1935 she hires the architects Hans Ostler and Max Ott to build the house. Photo: Gunda Lexer

Otto Mayer, chancellor of the International Olympic Committee.

Professor Carl Diem, general secretary of the organization committee for the Berlin Olympics, commissions her in 1935 to make the "Olympia" films.

In strahlender La

[Hitler] said amiably, but earnestly: 'Party Member Hess has told me why you wish to speak to me. I can assure you that your worries are groundless. You will have no problem this time.' 'That is not all, my Führer. I am afraid I cannot make this film … I am completely unfamiliar with all the subject matter. I can't even tell the SA from the SS.' 'That's an advantage. Then you'll see only the essentials. I don't want a boring Party rally film; I don't want newsreel shots. I want an artistic visual document. The Party people don't understand this. Your *Blue Light* proved that you can do it.' … Then he said, smiling, but in a resolute tone, ' … Don't worry, and don't force me to keep asking you. It's only six days you'll be giving me … you have to have more self-confidence. You can and you will do this project.' It sounded almost like an order. I realized that I could not break Hitler's resolve." She films with a crew of 18 cameramen and their assistants, among them, once again, Sepp Allgeier, Franz Weihmayr, Walter Riml, and Walter Frentz. The cameramen experiment with innovative techniques and angles: they film Hitler's speech to the Hitler Youth with a moving camera that moves about the rostrum on a curved track, and they use roller skates in filming several scenes. On a 125-foot-tall flagpole in the Luitpold Grove, Albert Speer had a special elevator contructed that would allow Leni Riefenstahl to film the mass parades as a whole. Some 400,000 feet of footage are produced in all, more than 100 hours. Leni Riefenstahl needs five months of intensive work to review the footage, edit it, and synchronize the music for *Triumph of the Will*. Not all of the events of the party rally appear in the film; for example, the Congress of National Socialist Women and the army are not shown. The director is not concerned with the chronology and exact documentation of the event but rather with its atmosphere, mood, and inner rhythm. She achieves a "symphonic arrangement" by editing the documentary images much as she does her feature films. Thus she dispenses with any commentary and dramatizes the course of events by crosscutting scenes. The sound-track combines sound from the actual events with film music by Herbert Windt. One problem that arises with the recordings results from the different speeds used by the cameramen in shooting, because cameras at the time are still cranked by hand, so that with the rapid changes in images the conductor is unable to change the tempo at the same pace. In the end, Leni Riefenstahl conducts the orchestra herself, because she knows every scene so precisely. But even during the editing of *Triumph of the Will*, there are conflicts. Rainy weather results in footage of the army that Leni Riefenstahl considers far too bad to include in her film. General Walter von Reichenau is outraged that the army, which has taken part in the party rally for the first time, will not appear in the film at all and complains to Hitler. But the director refuses, because it would destroy the artistic integrity of her film. As a compromise she proposes making a short film of the army at the next party rally. The result is the 28-minute film *Day of Freedom! – Our Armed Forces!* realized in Nuremberg in September 1935. A camera crew of five members is hired for the work, including Willy Zielke, Hans Ertl, Walter Frentz, Guzzi Lantschner, and Albert Kling. The only thing they have to shoot is the army exercises, which take place on a single day. The camera crew does outstanding work, and it is especially the film's form, for which Leni Riefenstahl gives Willy Zielke responsibility, that satisfies the army.

1935

Professor Carl Diem and the International Olympic Committee offer her a chance to make a documentary on the Eleventh Olympic Games, which will take place in

In late July 1936 she flies to Greece with a small film crew to film the lighting of the Olympic flame. Photo: Weltbild

In the plane en route to Athens, late July 1936. She discusses the filming in Olympia with her cameramen.

With her cameramen Hans Ertl (center) and Walter Frentz (right) in the sports arena during the Berlin Olympics, August 1936.

With a viewfinder, August 1936. Photo: Binder

Germany for the first time in 1936. Diem is the secretary general of the organization committee for the Olympics and a well-known German functionary in the sports world until the 1950s. At first she hesitates, because she does not really want to make any more documentary films, but in the end she accepts because she is attracted to the idea of shaping the various contests into a film that is convincing both from the point of view of art and that of sports. Arnold Fanck had already made the film *Das weisse Stadion* (The White Stadium, 1928) about the Winter Olympic Games in St. Moritz. The Olympics are broadcast on television and comprehensively covered on radio for the first time. Leni Riefenstahl signs a contract with the Tobis film company, which offers an enormous guarantee of 1.5 million reichsmarks. For the production of the film she establishes Olympia-Film – with herself and her brother, Heinz, as the partners – with financial support from the propaganda ministry of the Reich through the Film Credit Bank. For tax reasons, her firm functions in trust for the Reich.

1936

In preparation for the *Olympia* film, she visits the Winter Olympic Games in Garmisch-Partenkirchen and hires 42 cameramen, including Walter Frentz, Guzzi Lantschner, Hans Ertl, and Willy Zielke, who directed the experimental film *Das Stahltier* (The Steel Animal, 1934–1935). In the months before the Games begin the camera crew is given a special training session, in which they practice capturing on film the rapid movements of the contests and the athletes in training, experiment with various camera positions, and test film stocks. A small film crew travels with Leni Riefenstahl in July to Greece in order to film the lighting of the Olympic flame in the grove of Olympia. Because cars block the altar, the scene is later redone using a

With Walter Traut, her most important colleague, she prepares for the shooting at the sports arena. He is the executive secretary of her production company, Olympia- Film, as well as director of production of the documentary film.

Every night in Ruhwald Castle in Berlin, the filming is discussed. She evaluates the film shot that day and reassigns her camera crew for the next day's shooting.

For the Vienna premiere of "Olympia" in April 1938 she is honored with a banquet at the Hofburg.

torch bearer at the Kurisch Spit on the Baltic Sea. There, too, Willy Zielke shoots the scenes with the temple dancers, the javelin thrower, and the discus thrower that will later be seen in the prologue. On 1 August the Olympic Games open in Berlin. All 129 events that take place on six different sites in Berlin, Döberitz and Kiel are filmed. The crew consists of cameramen, assistants, drivers, three directors of photography, sound technicians, and technicians – about 150 people in all. Using a model of the stadium, the director establishes the various camera positions, and constant trips are made between the main headquarters of the crew in Ruhwald Castle, the stadium, and the processing studios, so that the film can be developed and tested the same day and the camera techniques can be discussed. The cameramen specialize in particular disciplines: Hans Ertl concentrates on running and swimming events; Walter Frentz films the sailing and the marathon; Guzzi Lantschner works with a handheld camera at the riding, gymnastics, swimming and rowing events; Kurt Neubert specializes in slow-motion shots; Hans Scheib works with the new 600-mm telephoto lens; and Leo de Laforgue takes candid shots of the audience using a miniature camera. Hans Ertl develops an underwater camera and a catapult camera for the sprints, though the judge will not allow him to use the latter. Despite violent resistance from the stadium officials, the director manages to get six pits dug from which the athletes in the sprinting and jumping contests can be filmed at unusual angles, for example framed against the sky. During training sessions the marathon runners, rowers, and military riders carry a wire basket with a miniature camera they can trigger themselves. The cameramen develop soundproof housings to reduce the noise from the cameras as well as tracks for moving shots, for example, around the wire cage of the hammer throwers. The rowing races

With Lutz Long, silver medal winner in the long jump, she watches the Olympic champion Jesse Owens make his record jump.

At the Italian premiere of "Olympia" in the Super-cinema theater in Rome in August 1938.

The Danish premiere of "Olympia" takes place in Copenhagen in August 1938 in the presence of the Danish royal couple.

At the premiere of "Olympia" in Copenhagen in August 1938.

are filmed from a bridge a hundred yards long, and everyday a balloon with a camera is released from the stadium to take shots of the whole spectacle. Towers are constructed for other interiors in the stadium: two in the middle of the stadium and one behind the starting point for the 100-meter dash. Cameras with speeds varying from 24 to 120 frames per second provide unusual slow-motion sequences. Many scenes are shot on location during the events, but some have to be redone later because of inadequate lighting: the 1,500-meter race from the decathlon and the pole vault, for example, which took place at night, and no floodlights were permitted during the Games. Certain especially difficult shots, like the final race of the swimmers, are made during the training races and later dubbed with the sound from the actual contest.

1937

For two years she reviews, archives and edits the film at the Geyer print lab in the Neukölln district of Berlin, where she has four editing rooms, a screening room, and a café – all with the latest technology. The amount of film shot is so large – 200 hours of film in all – that it seems hardly possible to manage an adequate editing job. Her goal is to create a film that is artistically satisfying but also interesting to nonathletes and viewers from all nations. She divides the material into two parts and uses the dramatic means of a feature film to transform the many contests, some of which are a little dull, in a way that is ambitious, engaging and rational. For example, using a montage of shots that were made of the high diving using three cameras filming at different speeds, she creates a flow of motion that makes the divers look like birds flying in the sky. The use of the camera varies between a straightforward documentary style and a more subjective one, while impressions and close-ups of the public create a mood of authenticity. For the soundtrack

During a press interview in Helsinki, summer 1938.

On the occasion of the premiere of the "Olympia" films in Oslo in August 1938, the Norwegian government honors the director with a banquet.

In front of the Royal Castle in Stockholm in August 1938. The Swedish King Gustav V grants her a private audience.

The International Olympic Committee awards her the Olympic Diploma for the "Olympia" films on 8 June 1939.

Leni Riefenstahl combines the film music by Herbert Windt and Walter Gronostay, the live sound from the competitions and spoken commentary. For the narration she hires, among others, the journalist Henri Nannen, who from 1948 will edit the magazine *Stern*. During the editing process she receives a visit from Goebbels, who advises her to cut the shots of the black athlete and repeated medal winner Jesse Owens. She refuses, just as later she will refuse when the French distributor proposes removing the shots of Hitler, because she rejects any intrusions into her artistic concept. *Schönheit im olympischen Kampf* (literally: Beauty in the Olympic Competition, published in 1994 in English as *Olympia*), a book of photographs in five languages, with numerous photographs of the Olympic Games and a foreword by Leni Riefenstahl, is published by the Deutscher Verlag in Berlin.

1938

The premiere of both *Olympia* films – *Festival of the People* and *Festival of Beauty* – takes place on 20 April, Hitler's 49th birthday, at the UFA-Palast am Zoo in Berlin. Leni Riefenstahl travels throughout Europe with the *Olympia* films and shows them with great success in Vienna, Graz, Paris, Brussels, Copenhagen, Stockholm, Helsinki, Oslo, Venice, Rome, and Bucharest. During her tour she gives lectures at Lund University, at the Deutsches Haus in Paris, and in Graz. In November she travels with the *Olympia* films to America to find a distributor there. On her arrival in New York she learns of the *Reichs-kristallnacht* ("Crystal Night"), the night between 9 and 10 November when many Jewish synagogues and other places of worship, graveyards, homes, and businesses are destroyed and more than 30,000 people are arrested. She refuses to believe the news and travels to New York, Chicago, Detroit, Los Angeles, Hollywood, Palm Springs, and San Francisco. But the Anti-Nazi League

Publicity still of Gustaf Gründgens in the role of Hamlet, with a handwritten dedication dated 11 November 1939.

Before beginning the filming of "Penthesilea" the director relaxes on Capri.

In the Alps in August 1939. A few days later World War II breaks out.

During the filming of "Tiefland" in the Dolomites. The crew films several times on the Rosengarten massif between 1940 and 1942.

and many German émigrés, including Fritz Lang, turn against performances of the *Olympia* films in America. She meets the producer Walt Disney, the automobile manufacturer Henry Ford, and the director King Vidor, and despite the protest, she manages to conclude a distribution agreement with the firm British Gaumont before returning home.

1939

Back in Europe, she gives a lecture in Paris in February on the topic "Is Film Art?" in which she advances the view that image and motion are the main criteria of the artistic film. She concentrates on her film project *Penthesilea* and in the spring she establishes the firm Leni Riefenstahl-Film for its production. Arnold Fanck will later work for her company and direct films for the chief building inspection program under the direction of Albert Speer, including films about the most important sculptors of the Third Reich, Josef Thorak and Arno Breker. Parallel with Leni Riefenstahl-Film and Reichsparteitag-Film, Olympia-Film will continue to exist until January 1942 and, from the enormous amount of material not used in the *Olympia* films, will produce about 20 sports films under the direction of Guzzi Lantschner, Harald Reinl and Joachim Bartsch that are distributed as shorts. Leni Riefenstahl writes the screenplay for *Penthesilea*, based on Heinrich von Kleist's tragedy, and hires both the crew and actors. Maria Koppenhöfer and Elisabeth Flickenschildt, known especially as stage actresses, are chosen as the priestesses. The extras hired to play Amazons are given riding lessons. Leni Riefenstahl, too, prepares for the leading role, taking speech lessons and learning to ride bareback. The filming is scheduled to take place in the Libyan desert and on Sylt Island or at the Kurisch Spit. For the desert shots, the Italian governor general of Libya, Marshall Italo Balbo, promises her 1,000 white horses with Libyan riders. To

The actress Henny Porten visits the village set in Krün, near Mittenwald, fall 1940.
Photo: Dufling

Mountain climbing in the Dolomites, circa 1940.

Her brother, Heinz, 1942. He works as the head engineer in their father's firm. In July 1944, at the age of 38, he dies in battle in Russia.
Photo: Rolf Lantin

She marries Peter Jacob on 21 March 1944 in Kitzbühel. Her husband, now a major in the mountain troops, received special permission to marry, and he returns to the front just a few days after the wedding.

For her role in "Penthesilea" she learns to ride.

direct the scenes in which she is acting she chooses Jürgen Fehling, who is working at the Prussian State Theater on the Gendarmenmarkt in Berlin under Gustaf Gründgens. With the outbreak of the war, work on the costly project is halted. Just a few days after the start of the war on 1 September, Leni Riefenstahl and many of her colleagues from her production company offer their services to the army to produce war reportage. They travel to Końskie in Poland in order to produce weekly newsreels from General von Reichenau's section of the front. One day after her arrival, at a funeral for German soldiers killed the day before by Polish partisans, she witnesses German soldiers massacring Polish civilians and in disgust she immediately ceases her activity as a war correspondent. The Tobis production company picks up the *Tiefland* project again, which had been called off by Terra in 1934. Leni Riefenstahl works with Harald Reinl, whom she knew as an actor in Fanck films, on the script for six weeks. They hope to get Brigitte Horney or Hilde Krahl to star as Martha the Gypsy, but neither is available. Finally, the director decides to play the leading role herself. The Spanish nobleman Don Sebastian is played by the stage actor Bernhard Minetti, a member of Gustaf Gründgens's ensemble at the Preussisches Staatstheater in Berlin, who is only released for the role after long negotiations. For the role of Pedro, a shepherd in the Pyrenees, she finds, after a long search, the amateur actor Franz Eichberger, whom she meets by chance at a ski race and who emanates precisely the sort of innocence that she feels the professional actors lack. After the test shots, Tobis accepts him, despite his heavy dialect, and he is given training in acting and diction.

1940

The beginning of the war on the western front means that *Tiefland* cannot be filmed,

The director and her husband in the fall of 1945 in the Seebichl House near Kitzbühel. The French occupying forces place the couple under house arrest for several weeks.

The American judge Michael A. Musmanno, who also took part in the Nuremberg Trials of 1945–1946, informs Leni Riefenstahl in Garmisch, spring 1948, that the alleged diaries of Eva Braun that Luis Trenker published are forgeries.

With Hanni Isele, her secretary of many years.

as originally planned, in the Pyrenees; consequently, she has the village, the castle, and the mill for the film built in Krün near Mittenwald, in the Karwendel Mountains. In mid-September the village for the film is ready, and it becomes a tourist attraction. The mountain scenes are filmed on the Rosengarten massif in the Dolomites. The plan is to complete the outdoor scenes by the end of autumn, but they are repeatedly delayed owing to scheduling difficulties with the actors, the camera crew being drafted into the army, problems with animals, and the director's illness. During the filming in Mittenwald she meets Peter Jacob, first lieutenant in the mountain troops, whom she will later marry.

1941–1944

The filming of *Tiefland* is supposed to continue in January 1941 in the Babelsberg studios, where the film architects Erich Grave and Isabella Ploberger have recreated the interior of the castle. On orders from the Ministry of Propaganda, however, the studios have to be freed up to begin shooting films important to the war effort. In Berlin she experiences her first air raid. She rehearses her dance scenes with Harald Kreutzberg. Despite her illness, filming begins in the studio at first under the direction of G. W. Pabst and is then later continued by Arthur Maria Rabenalt. In the summer of 1942 filming continues in the Dolomites with a she-wolf that the Berlin zoologist Dr. Bernhard Grzimek has trained especially for the film. On her 40th birthday she becomes engaged to Peter Jacob. In the spring of 1943 she finally receives the currency for the filming in Spain. From a cattle breeder near Salamanca she borrows 600 bulls bred for bull fighting, which are then driven to a mountain range near Madrid for the filming. After the shooting has been completed, she returns to Berlin, which is now subjected to constant air raids.

Portrait, 1948.
Photo: Walter Frentz

With her mother, Bertha Riefenstahl (here at the age of 84) she lives in a small apartment in the Schwabing district of Munich from 1950 on.

In Rome in 1953 she visits the actress Gina Lollobrigida on the set of "Bread, Love, and Dreams" (1953) by Luigi Comencini.

With Roberto Rosselli[ni], one of the founders of neorealism in cinema.
Photo: G. B. Poletto/La Stampa

The Italian director and actor Vittorio De Sica meets with her in Rome in 1953. He wants to take the lead in her film project "The Red Devils".

She marries Peter Jacob on 21 March 1944 in Kitzbühel in a war wedding. On 30 March 1944 she meets Hitler at the Berghof for the last time, when he invites her and her husband Major Jacob. In July her father, Alfred Riefenstahl, dies in Berlin at the age of 65, and on 20 July her brother, Heinz, dies in a punishment battalion on the Russian front. In the autumn the final studio shots for *Tiefland* are completed in a studio in Prague. Filming has taken more than four years. In November 1944 Leni Riefenstahl evacuates together with her crew to Seebichl House near Kitzbühel, where she has her own editing, mixing and projection rooms built in order to complete work on the film *Tiefland*. Some of the copies, films and takes are stored in two bunkers in the Johannisthal district of Berlin.

1945

Her mother, Bertha, leaves Berlin in February and arrives at Seebichl House. From now on she will live with her daughter. When the Americans occupy the Tyrol in spring, Leni Riefenstahl is arrested and brought to the Dachau prisoner-of-war camp of the U.S. Seventh Army. The former concentration camp now holds leading National Socialists, including Hermann Göring. During the hearings she is confronted with photographs from concentration camps for the first time and is deeply affected. On 3 June the U.S. Army grants her permission to return to Kitzbühel. In the summer the French take over the occupation of the northern Tyrol and Vorarlberg. Owing to power struggles between the nationalistically inclined military government and the Communist Sûreté – the police for public security – Leni Riefenstahl is taken into custody several times, released again, and then finally placed under arrest. Her bank account is frozen, her house is seized and all her property, including her archive of film and photography, is taken to Paris.

At the opening of Film Casino in Munich in 1954 she meets the French actor Jean Marais (far left).

Ten years after completing the filming of "Tiefland" she reunites with its star, Franz Eichberger (right), at the premiere of the film on 11 February 1954 at the EM-Theater in Stuttgart.
Photo: Bruno Arnold

1946–1947

In early April 1946 she is sent to the French-controlled zone in Germany. With her mother, her husband and several colleagues, she is brought first, as a prisoner under police guard, to Breisach near Freiburg in the Black Forest. In August they are quartered in Königsfeld in the Black Forest. She is prohibited from leaving the area. Peter Jacob works as a wine salesman to earn the family income. In the spring of 1947 she divorces her husband after he is unfaithful to her. Leni Riefenstahl's situation is difficult: she suffers from depression. Against her will, she is placed by the French military government in the secured section of the Freiburg psychiatric clinic from May to August 1947 and treated with electroshock therapy.

1948

In early February, at the instigation of her lawyer in Paris, the French military government of the state of Baden overturns the arrest. The release of her confiscated property is, however, delayed when the alleged diary of Eva Braun, Hitler's lover, is published in the French newspaper *France Soir* and later in the German newspaper *Wochenende*. Luis Trenker vouches for the accuracy of the diary, which depicts pornographic scenes between Leni Riefenstahl and Hitler. Eva Braun's eldest sister sues the German publisher Olympia-Verlag; Leni Riefenstahl takes part as a joint plaintiff. The court judges that the diary was forged – this is the first of more than 50 court cases that Leni Riefenstahl will be involved in, under right to legal aid, over the coming years. She continues the struggle for the release of the footage confiscated from her, which she will not regain until 1953. The Olympic Committee sends her Olympic Diploma for the *Olympia* films by mail, because she is not granted a travel visa for the award ceremony in Lausanne. United Artists shows the *Olympia* films in the Unit-

Her first film project after the war, "Black Freight", deals with the modern slave trade in East and Central Africa. The grueling filming takes place in autumn 1956 in Queen Elizabeth National Park in West Uganda.

In April 1956 she travels to Africa for the first time. A year earlier she had read Hemingway's "The Green Hills of Africa" with enthusiasm.

After a long search, she finds warriors of the Jalau tribe in Kisumu on Lake Victoria to use as extras for "Black Freight".

Two Nuba wrestlers from the southern Sudan. She sees this photograph in a back issue of "Stern" while spending six weeks in the hospital in Nairobi recovering from an auto accident in the spring of 1956.
© George Rodger/Magnum/Agentur Focus

ed States for the first time. They appear under the title *Kings of the Olympics* and are later shown as educational films at American universities.

1949

Manfred George writes to her from New York. From this point on they will remain in constant contact by letter, and several times he will offer to write her biography. In May an article appears in the Munich-based magazine *Revue*, in which she is accused of having forced Gypsies from a concentration camp to work as extras in the film *Tiefland*. She sues editor Helmut Kindler for defamation of character. The court comes to the conclusion that the Maxglan Camp was not a concentration camp but a reception camp for Gypsies and that Leni Riefenstahl was never at the camp. The Gypsies were selected there by Harald Reinl. Thus she wins the suit, but it is taken up again in 1982. In the autumn, the Finnish Olympic Committee asks her to make a film about the 1952 summer Olympics in Helsinki, while the Norwegians make a similar request for the winter games. She turns both down because she believes she cannot improve on her *Olympia* films. On 16 December she is judged a "fellow traveler" in her third hearing in the denazification process (the French military government challenged two previous judgments that placed her in the classification "law not applicable" – i.e., innocent). This judgment is upheld by the ruling court in Berlin in April 1952, so that she once again has control over her private property in Berlin, though her house in Dahlem had been completely rebuilt in the meantime without her permission.

1950–1952

With her mother she moves into Tengstrasse in the Schwabing district of Munich in 1950, where she begins film work again. In Fregene, near Rome, she writes for the Italian

With her life partner, Horst Kettner, she returns to her Nuba friends in Tadoro in the winter of 1968.

Horst Kettner with an Arriflex camera, around 1968.

The Sudanese president Gaafar Muhammad al-Nimeiry decorates her in 1976 for her two books of photographs of the Nuba.

film company Capital Pictures a treatment for the ski film *The Red Devils*, which is a variation on the Penthesilea theme and is planned as a color film. Financial difficulties cause the company to pull out of the project in 1951. This puts a stop to it for the moment, but the director continues, despite interruptions, to work on the project until 1954. She meets film directors Vittorio De Sica and Roberto Rossellini in Rome. As representatives of neorealism, they have high regard for her film work because she has been among the first to shoot on location. Together with the Austrian general consul in Rome, she founds Iris-Film, in order to produce a remake of *The Blue Light,* as the original negative had been sold by Harry Sokal in America, without her permission. She edits a new version from the unused footage that has survived. The French director and artist Jean Cocteau writes her a letter in 1952; they meet and become friends.

1953

The footage that had been confiscated by the French is returned to the director. It includes the original negatives of the *Olympia* films and copies of the mountain films. She receives also the footage for *Tiefland,* but it is completely cut up and damaged. In order to produce *Tiefland* again, she founds Junta-Film, in Vienna, together with her former cameraman Otto Lantschner, but she is only able to restore the film partially. She wants to engage Herbert von Karajan as conductor and the Vienna Symphonic Orchestra to record the music, but cannot afford his fee.

1954

Following the premiere of *Tiefland* on 11 February at the EM-Theater in Stuttgart, she travels through Austria with Franz Eichberger, the actor who played the shepherd Pedro, and presents the film. Jean Cocteau, president of the jury at the Cannes Film Festival,

requests to no avail that *Tiefland* be submitted belatedly as the German entry for the festival. The film is shown in Cannes unofficially. Once again, she concentrates on her work on the film project *The Red Devils*, which is planned to be filmed primarily in the Austrian Alps. Vittorio De Sica, Jean Marais, and the still-unknown Brigitte Bardot are planned for the main roles, as well as the best ski racers of the time, including the Austrian Andreas Molterer. She negotiates a coproduction with the Austrian government and the Austrian Credit Bank, who expect the film to promote tourism. When the Vienna newspaper *Der Abend* accuses the government of financing a German film with Austrian tax money, the film project comes to a definitive end though Herbert Tischendorf, who also produced the *Sissi* films, wants to finance the film.

1955

She works on several scripts, none of which can be made, however. Among others, she writes *Three Stars on the Cloak of the Madonna* for Anna Magnani as well as *Frederick the Great and Voltaire* – in collaboration with Jean Cocteau, who intends to play both roles under Leni Riefenstahl's direction. She travels to Spain, with various treatments for films about Spain. Back in Munich she reads with great enthusiasm in a single night Hemingway's autobiographical travel journal *Green Hills of Africa*. She fascinated with Africa for a time, and when she happens to come across an article in the *Süddeutsche Zeitung* on modern slavery in Africa, it reinforces her idea of making a film in Africa. Together with Helge Pawlinin, a director at the Munich Kammerspiele, she writes a treatment for *Black Freight*, a film on the modern slave trade. She plans to take the leading role herself. Gloria Film Distribution briefly shows an interest in *Black Freight*. The company insists that all the roles – even the Arab

Facing page: Leni Riefenstahl frequently returns to her friends in Tadoro. Here she is shown in 1974 with the Arriflex camera.

With the Mesakin Quissayr Nuba of Tadoro, 1974.

In the editing room in her house in Pöcking on Lake Starnberg, 1988. Here she is archiving the Nuba footage.

August Arnold (1898–1983) – director and coowner of Arnold & Richter, a Munich company specializing in film technology – her close friend since the 1950s. In 1967 he wins an Oscar for the invention of the first industrially produced 35-mm single lens reflex camera.

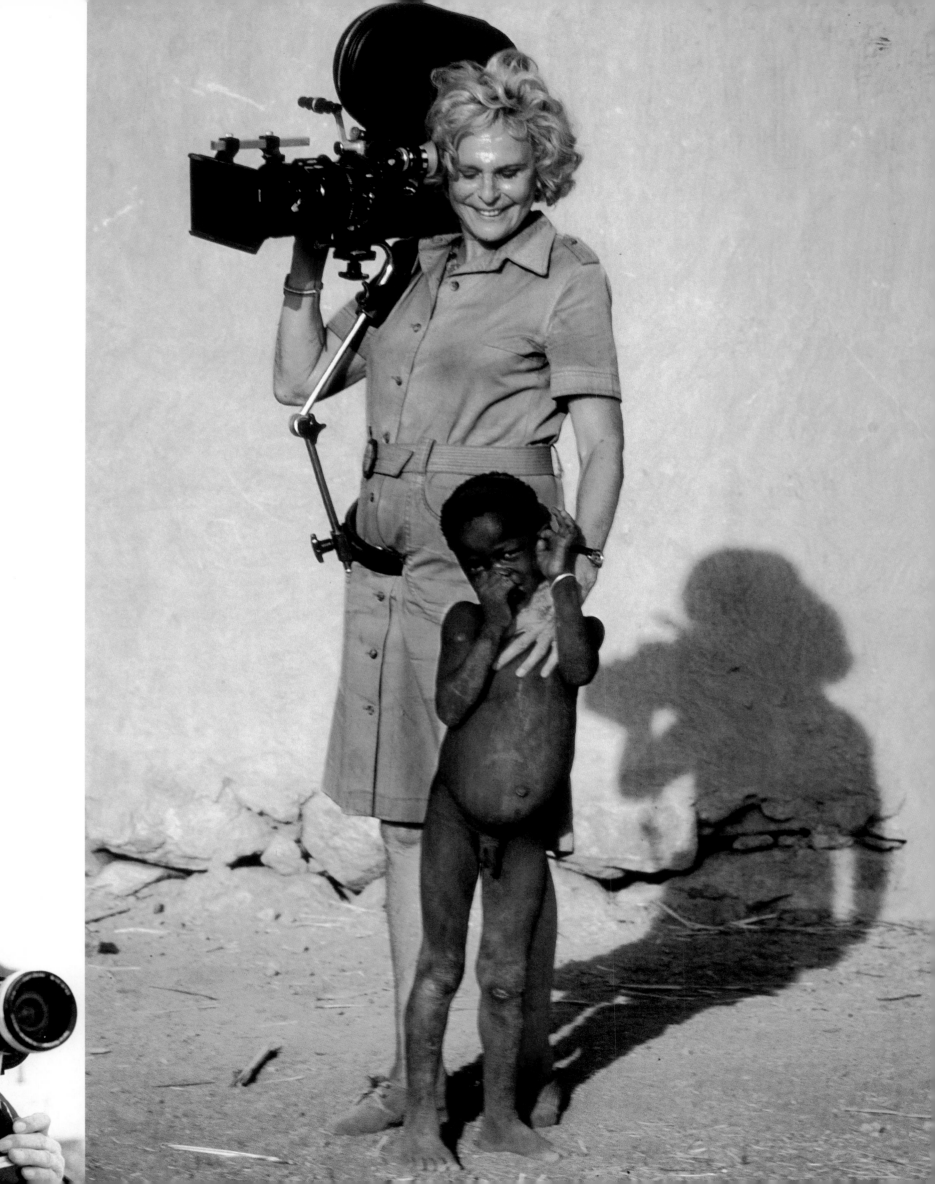

slave dealers and the slaves – must be played by German actors. The director adamantly refuses. In the end, they agree on the stars – O. E. Hasse and Winnie Markus or Ruth Leuwerik. However, one of the directors of the distribution company vetoes the project.

1956–1957

Nevertheless, she decides to travel to Africa on her own – at the age of 54. In Kenya she makes contact with Lawrence-Brown Safaris, which arranged the dangerous animal scenes for *King Solomon's Mines* (1950) and *The Snows of Kilimanjaro* (1952). During a exploratory trip she is involved in a serious car accident, which she barely survives, and spends six weeks in a hospital in Nairobi. Lawrence-Brown Safaris becomes interested in the film project and offers to collaborate and provide equipment at its own expense. Together with her former colleague Walter Traut, who is now running a production company and has produced the films *08/15* (1954–1955) and *The Physician of Stalingrad* (1958) among others, she founds Stern-Film. As with her first movie, *The Blue Light*, her budget is very low, and she can only manage the project by arranging to defer payment to the investors and crew. In August 1956 she begins the search in Kenya for locations and extras. Because of the Suez crisis, the ship transporting the equipment has to make a detour via South Africa, and so it arrives several weeks late. The shooting is delayed; she flies to Munich to show the test shots to possible partners. But no contract results. In the meanwhile the African extras return home, and Lawrence-Brown Safaris confiscates the equipment she has borrowed as security. With that, this project too comes to an end.

1958

The *Olympia* films are shown with great success in film clubs in Berlin, Bremen, and Hamburg. In order to show them publicly,

the director must, at the insistence of the Voluntary Self-Supervision Board of the German Film Industry, remove all of the scenes that show Hitler or the German victory celebrations. Twenty years after the premiere of the films, the naked upperbody of a dancer in the prologue has to be darkened with a shadow so that the film can be shown to minors.

1959

The first retrospective of her films takes place at the Venice Biennale. The board of the festival demands the unabridged version of the *Olympia* films. In Venice, after nearly 30 years, she meets Josef von Sternberg again, and they see each other daily, so she learns much about this experiences in America with Marlene Dietrich. The English company Adventure Film, led by Philip Hudsmith, offers to remake *The Blue Light*. The plan is for a dance film in the style of *The Red Shoes* (1948) using the new 70-mm Super Technirama process. The English writer W. Somerset Maugham is first considered to write the screenplay, then later the founder of the Scientology sect, L. Ron Hubbard. She hires the actors Pier Angeli and Laurence Harvey, who was nominated for an Oscar in 1958. Her partners withdraw, however, when journalists protest against the director at a press conference in London in January 1960.

1960–1961

In 1960 she files suit for copyright infringement against the Swedish company Minerva Film which produced Erwin Leiser's film *Mein Kampf*. In his compilation Leiser used without permission about a thousand feet of film from *Triumph of the Will*, integrated with photographs from concentration camps. Although the initial judgment is in her favor, while she is in the Sudan, in 1969 the Federal Supreme Court in Karlsruhe decides that *Triumph of the Will* was financed by the Nazi Party and not, as she claims, on her own,

Facing page: At the Indian Ocean, 1974. She enjoys the athletic aspect of diving in the Indian Ocean, where the surf is very high.

As a diver, 1986. Leni Riefenstahl is now considered the oldest diver in the world.

During filming in the Maldive Islands. Horst Kettner accompanies her on her trips to the most beautiful diving regions of the world.

In the Maldive Islands, 1997.

without any assistance from the party, through a distribution agreement with the UFA. Disappointed by this judgment, she searches for witnesses who can disprove the decision. She turns to Arnold Raether, former head of the film department of the Nazi party and once one of her biggest opponents. She is able to persuade him to make a notarized statement that the Nazi party did not invest any money and that Goebbels forbade any support for the film. According to Leni Riefenstahl, this document could secure her the sole rights to her film *Triumph of the Will*. In Paris she successfully sues Plon, the publisher of the book *Six Million Dead*, about Adolf Eichmann's crimes against European Jews. Its author, Victor Alexandrov, falsely claims in one chapter that Leni Riefenstahl made several films in concentration camps for Eichmann.

1962

When Leni Riefenstahl learns that the Nansen Society, a German scientific organization, wants to make a documentary film in the Southern Sudan, she asks to be included and promises in return to make a film about the Nansen Society project. She takes part in the expedition. During her hospital stay in Nairobi in 1956 she had seen, in a back issue of *Stern*, a photograph by George Rodger that showed two athletic Nuba wrestlers from the southern Sudan. Ever since, the image has not left her. In the southern Sudan, however, there are constant battles between Muslims and Christians, Arabs and black Africans, so that travel to the so-called closed districts requires a special permit. In October the members of the Nansen expedition fly to Khartoum. Because bad weather prevents the group from taking the direct route to the Nuer tribe, Leni Riefenstahl is able to persuade them to take the route over the Nuba Mountains in the region of Kordofan. After crossing arduous sand dunes, the expedition reaches the isolated Nuba village of Tadoro

In 1974 Mick and Bianca Jagger insist on Leni Riefenstahl as the photographer for a portrait in the London "Sunday Times Magazine".

At the Munich Olympic Games in 1972 she photographs for the London "Sunday Times Magazine". After the Games, the photographs are juxtaposed in an article with photographs from the Berlin Olympics of 1936.

She has been friends with the actress and writer Hildegard Knef since 1972.

With Albert Speer and the historian Joachim C. Fest in 1972 she takes part in the semidocumentary film "Erinnerungen an einen Sommer in Berlin" (Memories of a Summer in Berlin) by Rolf Hädrich, based on a chapter of a novel by Thomas Wolfe dealing with the 1936 Olympics.

With Mick Jagger, London, 1974.

in mid-December and sets up camp there for seven weeks. Leni Riefenstahl quickly makes friends with the initially shy villagers, learns their language, lives with them, and photographs them. In Tadoro she sees a wrestling contest that carries ritual significance for the Mesakin Quissayr Nuba, and she is taken to the *seribe,* a herd camp, where only Nuba men are allowed to stay.

1963

The Nansen Society leaves her, and she travels on alone. In April she accompanies the governor of the Upper Nile Province on a 14-day inspection trip and photographs the Anuak, Murle, Nuer, and Dinka tribes. In late May she undertakes a photo safari to the Masai in Laitokitok on Kilimanjaro, where she witnesses initiation rites. On her ten-month journey, traveling alone and without a tent, she shoots 210 rolls of film, but back in Germany she discovers that most of the film has deteriorated. She gives very successful slide lectures on her experiences in Africa.

1964

A retrospective of her work has successful runs in Bremen. During the Winter Olympics in Innsbruck she takes photographs for the Olympia-Verlag. She gives slide lectures at Harvard University, at Kodak's George Eastman House in Rochester, and at *National Geographic Magazine* and the National Geographic Society in Washington, D.C. The American film company Odyssey Productions offers money for a film about the Nuba. Shortly before her departure in early November, she hears on the radio that a civil war has broken out in the Sudan. She decides to continue the expedition anyway and sets off with two drivers. In Khartoum the street fighting is intensifying, but she receives permission to visit the southern Sudan and film there. She spends Christmas back in Tadoro with the Nuba.

Portrait of Mick Jagger, London, 1974. Photo: Leni Riefenstahl

She meets Pop artist Andy Warhol in New York in 1974. She is struck by the atmosphere of the Factory.

With the Japanese director Kenji Ono.

1965

On 14 January her mother Bertha Riefenstahl, with whom she has been living since 1945 and whom she loves deeply, dies. She immediately halts the expedition and flies to Munich for the funeral. Afterward she hires the young cameraman Gerhard Fromm. Back in Tadoro, she films Nuba wrestling matches, ritual acts, dances, and everyday life. While filming she gets too close to the wrestlers, and they fall on her in the struggle, breaking two of her ribs. Back in Munich she turns in the film stock – the new, especially light-sensitive ER Stock – for development, but it is returned in an unusable state with a green cast. This puts an end to her Nuba film for the time being.

1966

The Nuba photographs appear for the first time in *African Kingdom*, a book of photographs published by Time Life Books. The Museum of Modern Art and the George Eastman House present retrospectives of the films by and with Leni Riefenstahl. In November she is visited by Albert Speer, minister of armaments and war production during the Third Reich, who has been released from Spandau prison in Berlin after serving 20 years for war crimes. From this point on she will remain in close contact with him. In December she travels to the Sudan for 28 days and celebrates Christmas with her friends in Tadoro for the third time. She considers living with them permanently.

1967–1968

The Austrian Film Museum in Vienna presents a Leni Riefenstahl Film Week in 1967, showing five of her films. She prepares a new expedition to the Sudan, and in order to raise money she gives slide lectures and interviews, for the Italian broadcasting company RAI and the BBC, among others. During preparations for the trip she meets Horst Kettner. He accompanies her as a camera assistant on all her trips from now on and becomes her life partner. They spend Christmas 1968 with the Mesakin Quissayr Nuba and show them 8-mm films of Charlie Chaplin, Harold Lloyd and Buster Keaton.

1969

The ruined photographs of 1965 are to be reshot. But civil war, the dress code forbidding nakedness (imposed by the Muslim government) and tourism have affected the traditions and living conditions of the Nuba, and it is difficult to find the shots she hoped for. Back in Germany Leni Riefenstahl and the art director Rolf Gillhausen choose photographs for a 15-page series of images in *Stern* magazine.

1970–1972

She travels repeatedly with Horst Kettner to East Africa. In 1971 in Malindi on the Indian Ocean she hears of snorkeling for the first time and joins a group of divers. The BBC airs the *Olympia* films during the Olympic Games in Munich in 1972. She photographs the Games for the *Sunday Times Magazine*, which in an article after the Olympics juxtaposes the photographs with others from 1936. At a reception at the American Embassy she meets Jesse Owens again.

1973

Her first collection of photographs of the Nuba is published by Paul-List-Verlag in Munich, with a title that translates as *The Nuba: Like People from Another Star* (published in 1974 in English as *The Last of the Nuba*). The subtitle of the German edition was Albert Speer's suggestion; Leni Riefenstahl did the layout and wrote the texts. The publishers Tom Stacey, Harper & Row, and Denoël withdraw on short notice from the planned international copublication; Paul-List-Verlag takes the risk of publishing it alone. The

For her 75th birthday she is presented with copies of a 45-year correspondence with Professor Koichi Okajimi. Ever since he saw "The Blue Light" for the first time, they remained in constant contact by letter. To the left of Leni Riefenstahl is her publisher, Robert Schäfer, of the Munich-based Paul-List-Verlag.
© Christine Strub

With the actor Horst Buchholz on her 80th birthday. She presents her fourth book of photographs, "Leni Riefenstahl's Africa", for which she also wrote the text and did the layout.

With mountain climber and extreme sports athlete Reinhold Messner on her 85th birthday.

book is a great success and appears – as do almost all of the following books of photographs – later in America, Great Britain, France, Italy, and Japan. She travels with Horst Kettner to Mombasa and Malindi and passes a diving test. To register for the diving course, she has to give the year of her birth as 1922 instead of 1902. When she announces that secret at the celebration for passing the test, she is much admired. She is fascinated with the world under water, the feeling of weightlessness, the beauty of the color and forms. The president of the Sudan, Gaafar Muhammad al-Nimeiry, grants her Sudanese citizenship in recognition of her services to the Sudan, she is the first female foreigner to be granted this honor. She asks him to ban harpooning in the Red Sea. On the return trip she dives in the Red Sea and photographs underwater for the first time.

1974

Leni Riefenstahl and Horst Kettner spend several weeks with the Mesakin Quissayr Nuba and show them the first Nuba book. Learning of the southeast Nuba and their traditional knife duels, they set out – with a limited supply of gasoline and without an accurate map – to find them. They manage to find the villages of Kau, Fungor, and Nyaro, where they can stay for just three days. They photograph the dances of the young girls, the knife duels and body paintings of the young men. Afterwards they travel to the Gulf of Honduras where they go diving off the island of Roatan and barely survive hurricane Fifi, in which eight to ten thousand people die. She is the guest of honor at the first Telluride Film Festival in Colorado. The festival opens with the film *The Blue Light* and presents all of the artist's other films as well. Together with the actress Gloria Swanson and the director Francis Ford Coppola she is honored with a silver medal for her artistic achievements.

1975

Together with Horst Kettner she spends five months with the southeast Nuba. She takes more than two thousand photographs of women being tattooed, men being painted, the knife duels of the young warriors and the *nyertun* dance festival. From October on the photographs begin to appear in magazines in Europe, America, Japan, Australia and Africa. The Art Director's Club in Germany awards her a gold medal for photography; the 20-page spread in *Stern,* designed by Rolf Gillhausen, wins a prize for the best layout. She travels to the Caribbean, including the Cayman and Virgin Islands, for diving. She photographs while diving during the day and at night and films underwater for the first time.

1976–1977

She is a guest of honor at the Summer Olympic Games in Montreal in 1976. The same year the BBC broadcasts for the first time excerpts of the film she took of the Nuba of Kau. Her second book of photographs is presented at the Frankfurt Book Fair of 1976 and published that same year under the English title *The People of Kau*; the photographer was responsible for the text and layout as well. Under contract from the magazine *GEO*, she travels again to the southeast Nuba in 1977. In the Sudan President Gaafar Muhammad al-Nimeiry decorates her in recognition of two books of Nuba photographs. In a television studio in Japan in 1977 she meets all of the Japanese athletes who participated in the 1936 Olympics, including the marathon winner Kitei Son. She and Horst Kettner make many diving trips to the Caribbean, the Indian Ocean and the Red Sea, where she films with a 16-mm camera for the first time.

1978–1981

Her first book of photographs of the undersea world is published in 1978 by Paul-List-

Her close colleague Gisela Jahn accompanies her to the celebration for her 90th birthday.

In 1992 she visits her friends Siegfried and Roy in Las Vegas.

Verlag and released in the same year under the English title *Coral Gardens*. She buys property in Pöcking, near Munich, where she has a prefabricated house set up. There she lives together with Horst Kettner. She fractures her femur in a ski accident at St. Moritz and is bedridden for a long time. Despite several operations, she suffers repeatedly from pain that only goes away when swimming or diving. In the following decades, Leni Riefenstahl and Horst Kettner make several diving trips to the Bahamas, the Caribbean, the Maldive Islands, Indonesia, Micronesia and Papua New Guinea. In 1980 Eiko Ishioka, an artist, internationally active art director and Oscar winner, organizes the exhibition *Nuba by Leni Riefenstahl* at the Seibu Museum of Art in Tokyo with 120 Nuba photographs, some of which are enlarged to sizes up to ten square yards.

1982–1989

The International Olympic Committee awards her a gold cup in 1982 in recognition of her *Olympia* films. Her book *Beauty in the Olympic Competition* (1937) is reprinted and also released in 1994 in London and New York under the title *Olympia*. On her 80th birthday she presents her fourth book of photographs, released in the same year under the English title *Leni Riefenstahl's Africa*, for which once again she wrote the text and did the layout. The book documents her many trips in East Africa and shows photographs of various tribes, including the Nuba, the Shilluk, the Masai, and others. After many unsuccessful attempts with ghost writers, she decides to write her memoirs herself. She begins on 1 November 1982 and finishes the book five years later. The archiving of the extensive documentary material and the writing itself are frequently interrupted by illness. The memoirs appear later in America, Great Britain, France, Spain, Italy, Sweden, and Japan.

1990–1992

In 1990 her second book of photographs is published by Herbig Verlag, and is also published one year later in England under the title *Wonders under Water*. At the Bunkamura Cultural Center in Tokyo in the winter of 1991–1992 Eiko Ishioka organizes the exhibition *Leni Riefenstahl: Life*, which presents the artist's complete oeuvre for the first time; it is enthusiastically received. Parts of the exhibition are shown in Kuopio, Finland, and Milan in 1996 and in Rome 1997.

1993

The three-hour documentary *The Wonderful, Horrible Life of Leni Riefenstahl* by Ray Müller, a German-English-Belgian coproduction, receives international awards, including an Emmy Award and the Japanese Special Prize of Film Critics.

1996

Johann Kresnik presents his choreographic play *Riefenstahl* at the Cologne Theater as part of his dance work concerned with historical figures. The two previous productions were *Ernst Jünger* and *Gründgens*.

1997

In Leipzig, a complete retrospective of her films is shown, for the first time in Germany. Leni Riefenstahl is the guest of honor at the Cinecon film festival in Los Angeles and receives the honorary prize of the festival.

1998

Time Magazine celebrates its 75th birthday at Radio City Music Hall in New York. The guests of honor include all the people still living who had ever appeared on the cover of the magazine. The only two German guests of honor are Leni Riefenstahl and Claudia Schiffer. The Film Museum in Potsdam shows *Leni Riefenstahl*, the artist's first solo show in Germany. The opening speech is given by

Facing page: The Bunkamura Cultural Center in Tokyo presents the first complete retrospective exhibition on the work of Leni Riefenstahl in 1991–1992. The art director and artist Eiko Ishioka initiates and designs the exhibition "Leni Riefenstahl: Life", which garners international attention.

In 1991 she meets Akio Morita, cofounder and chairman of Sony, in Tokyo.

She is the guest of honor at the film festival of the Cinecon association of film enthusiasts. She receives the honorary prize of the festival from the chairman of the association, Kevin John Charbeneau.

Dr. Albrecht Knaus, who published her memoirs in 1987, congratulates her on her 95th birthday.

her friend Kevin Brownlow, the British film journalist and director. A retrospective of her films runs parallel to the exhibition, which is extended.

1999

The pain from a slipped disc from which Leni Riefenstahl has long suffered becomes so unbearable that she must undergo a very risky operation in May. A hospital stay of eight weeks follows, during which she is treated with strong painkillers. Nevertheless, she soon takes up her work again. In December press agencies report that the American actress, producer, and director Jodie Foster is working on a film on the life of Leni Riefenstahl. Since 1987 several Hollywood stars, including Madonna, have been interested in the film rights. Odeon-Film in Munich is also interested in filming her life story. The plan is for a European coproduction together with Thomas Schühly, a former assistant of Rainer Werner Fassbinder; Schühly became known internationally for *The Deathmaker* (1995) and *The Name of the Rose* (1986).

2000

The play *Marleni: Preussische Diven blond wie Stahl* (literally: Marleni: Prussian Divas Blond as Steel) by Thea Dorn is performed at the Hamburg Theater. Under Jasper Brandis's direction the story tells of an imaginary meeting between Marlene Dietrich (Ilse Ritter) and Leni Riefenstahl (Marlen Diekhoff). In February the artist returns to the Nuba after 23 years to see whether her friends are still alive and to help them. She is accompanied by Ray Müller, who is making a second documentary film about her. During the filming the helicopter crashes from a height of 50 feet, and Leni Riefenstahl is taken to a Munich hospital, where she spends several weeks recovering from broken ribs and lung injuries. In May Leni Riefenstahl attends the opening at Camera Work gallery in Berlin for an exhibition of photographs that she took at the Olympic Games in 1936. The first exhibition of the artist's work in her native city attracts much attention. She continues work on various film and exhibition projects and plans new trips and diving expeditions.

Facing page: At the
Munich Film Ball, 2000
© Bogdan Kramliczek

The director Ray Müller
makes the documentary film
"The Wonderful, Horrible Life
of Leni Riefenstahl" (1993),
which wins prizes
internationally.

In spring 2000 Leni
Riefenstahl meets her
old friend Nuba chief
Gabike.

During the filming the
helicopter crashes from
a height of 50 feet and
turns over several times.

With broken ribs and
lung injuries Leni
Riefenstahl is taken to
the hospital of El-Obeid
in Sudan.

BÜCHER VON LENI RIEFENSTAHL
BOOKS BY LENI RIEFENSTAHL

Riefenstahl, Leni:
KAMPF IN SCHNEE UND EIS.
Hesse & Becker, Leipzig 1933.

Riefenstahl, Leni:
HINTER DEN KULISSEN DES REICHSPARTEITAGS-FILMS.
Franz Eher Nachfolge Verlag, München 1935.

Riefenstahl, Leni:
SCHÖNHEIT IM OLYMPISCHEN KAMPF
Mit einem Vorwort von Leni Riefenstahl, Dokumentation
zum Olympia-Film mit zahlreichen Aufnahmen von den
Olympischen Spielen 1936, Textunterschriften in Deutsch,
Französisch, Englisch, Spanisch und Italienisch, Original-
ausgabe im Deutschen Verlag (Ullstein-Verlag), Berlin
1937. Neuausgabe mit einem Geleitwort von Monique
Berlioux, Direktor des Internationalen Olympischen
Komitees, und einer Einführung von Kevin Brownlow,
Filmhistoriker und Filmmacher, Mahnert-Lueg Verlag,
München 1988.
English edition:
OLYMPIA
Documentation for the Olympia film with numerous
photographs of the Olympic Games 1936, foreword by
Monique Berlioux; introduction by Kevin Brownlow,
Quartet Books, London 1994.
OLYMPIA.
Documentation for the Olympia film with numerous
photographs of the Olympic Games 1936, foreword by
Monique Berlioux; introduction by Kevin Brownlow,
St. Martin's Press, New York 1994.

Riefenstahl, Leni:
DIE NUBA – MENSCHEN WIE VON EINEM ANDEREN STERN
Paul List Verlag, München 1973, ²1977. Ungekürzte
Neuausgabe als Taschenbuch im Deutschen Taschen Verlag,
München 1982; ungekürzte Neuausgabe als Taschenbuch
beim Ullstein Verlag, Frankfurt/Main, Berlin, Wien 1990.
English edition:
THE LAST OF THE NUBA
Harper & Row, New York 1974. New edition by
St. Martin's Press, New York 1995.
THE LAST OF THE NUBA
Collins, London 1976, ²1986.
Édition française:
LES NOUBA – DES HOMMES D'UNE AUTRE PLANÈTE
Traduit par Laurent Dispot, Chêne, Paris 1976.
Edición española:
LOS NUBA – HOMBRES COMO DE OTRO MUNDO
Lumen, Barcelona 1978.
Edició catalana:
ELS NUBA – HOMES D'UN ALTRE MÓN
Lumen, Barcelona 1978.
Edizione italiana:
I NUBA
Traduzione di Lia Volpatti, A. Mondadori, Milano
1978.

Japanese edition:
NUBA
Parco View Series, Parco Publishing Press, Tokyo 1980
& 1981. Paperback edition: Shincho-sha Press, Tokyo
1986.

Riefenstahl, Leni:
DIE NUBA VON KAU
Fotos, Text und Layout von Leni Riefenstahl,
Paul List Verlag, München 1976. Ungekürzte Neu-
ausgabe als Taschenbuch im Deutschen Taschen
Verlag, München 1982; ungekürzte Neuausgabe als
Taschenbuch beim Ullstein Verlag, Frankfurt/Main,
Berlin, Wien 1991.
DIE NUBA
Gemeinschaftsausgabe von „Die Nuba – Menschen
wie von einem anderen Stern" und „Die Nuba von Kau",
Komet, Frechen 2000.
English edition:
THE PEOPLE OF KAU
Photographs, text and layout by Leni Riefenstahl,
translated from the German by J. Maxwell Brownjohn,
Collins, London 1976.
THE PEOPLE OF KAU
Photographs, text and layout by Leni Riefenstahl,
translated from the German by J. Maxwell Brownjohn,
Harper & Row, New York 1976. New edition by
St. Martin's Press, New York 1997.
Édition française:
LES NOUBA DE KAU
Texte et photographies de Leni Riefenstahl, traduit par
Laurent Dispot, Chêne, Paris 1976, ²1997.
Edizione italiana:
GENTE DI KAU
Fotografie, layout e testo di Leni Riefenstahl, traduzione
di Lia Volpatti, A. Mondadori, Milano 1977.
Edición española:
LOS NUBA DE KAU
Fotografías, texto y maquetas de Leni Riefenstahl,
Lumen, Barcelona 1978.
Edició catalana:
ELS NUBA DE KAU
Fotografíes, text i maquetes de Leni Riefenstahl,
Lumen, Barcelona 1978.

Riefenstahl, Leni:
KORALLENGÄRTEN
Fotos, Text und Layout von Leni Riefenstahl,
Paul List Verlag, München 1978. Ungekürzte
Neuausgabe als Taschenbuch im Deutschen Taschen
Verlag, München 1982; ungekürzte Neuausgabe als
Taschenbuch beim Ullstein Verlag, Frankfurt/Main,
Berlin 1991.
English edition:
CORAL GARDENS
Photos, text and layout by Leni Riefenstahl, translated
by Elizabeth Walter, Collins, London 1978.
CORAL GARDENS
Photos, text and layout by Leni Riefenstahl, translated
by Elizabeth Walter, Harper & Row, New York 1978.

Édition française:
JARDINS DE CORAIL
Texte et photographies de Leni Riefenstahl, traduit par
Geneviève Dispout, Chêne, Paris 1978.
Edizione italiana:
GIARDINI DI CORALLO
Traduzione di Francesco Maria Bernardi, A. Mondadori,
Milano 1979.

Riefenstahl, Leni:
MEIN AFRIKA
Fotos, Text und Layout von Leni Riefenstahl, Paul List
Verlag, München 1982.
English edition:
LENI RIEFENSTAHL'S AFRICA
Photographs, text and layout by Leni Riefenstahl, translat-
ed by Kathrine Talbot, Collins, London 1982.
VANISHING AFRICA
Photographs, text and layout by Leni Riefenstahl, transla-
ted by Kathrine Talbot, Harmony Books, New York 1982.
Édition française:
L'AFRIQUE DE LENI RIEFENSTAHL
Texte et photographies de Leni Riefenstahl, traduit par
Louise Dupont, Herscher, Paris 1982.
Edizione italiana:
LA MIA AFRICA
Foto, testo e layout di Leni Riefenstahl, traduzione di
Fernando Solina, Mondadori, Milano 1983.

Riefenstahl, Leni:
MEMOIREN
Albert Knaus Verlag, München, Hamburg 1987.
Neuauflage in zwei Bänden, Herbig, München
1997; für das Taschenbuch neu eingerichtete
usgabe, Bd. I (1902–1945) und Bd. II (1945–1987)
beim Ullstein Verlag, Frankfurt/Main, Berlin 1990.
Edición española:
MEMORIAS
Prólogo de Román Gubern, traducción de Juan Godó
Costa, Lumen, Barcelona 1991.
Japanese edition:
MEMOIREN – THE GREATEST MEMOIR IN THE 20TH CENTURY
Bungei Shunju Press, Tokyo 1991, ²1995.
English edition:
THE SIEVE OF TIME: THE MEMOIRS OF LENI RIEFENSTAHL
Quartet Books, London 1992.
LENI RIEFENSTAHL: A MEMOIR
St. Martin's Press, New York 1993.
Paperback edition: Picador, New York 1995.
Edizione italiana:
STRETTA NEL TEMPO: STORIA DELLA MIA VITA
Altri Autori: Valtolina, Amelia, Bompiani, Milano 1995.
Finnish edition:
LENI RIEFENSTAHL
Editor Ritta Raatikainen, Viktor Barsokevitsch-senra,
Kuopio 1996.
Édition française:
MÉMOIRES
Traduction de l'allemand et postface par Laurent Dispot,
Grasset, Paris 1997.

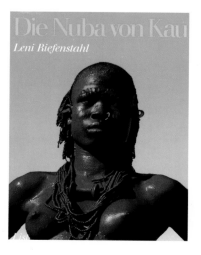

Riefenstahl, Leni:
WUNDER UNTER WASSER
Herbig Verlag, München 1990.
English edition:
WONDERS UNDER WATER
Quartet Books, London 1991.

AUSGEWÄHLTE ARTIKEL, DREHBERICHTE UND INTERVIEWS
MIT UND VON LENI RIEFENSTAHL
**SELECTED ARTICLES, SCRIPTS, AND INTERVIEWS
BY AND WITH LENI RIEFENSTAHL**

Riefenstahl, Leni:
DIE WEISSE ARENA.
Filmkurier, 17. Februar 1928.

Riefenstahl, Leni:
MAN FRIERT SICH DURCH.
Die Filmwoche, Nr. 44, 30. Oktober 1929.

Riefenstahl, Leni:
DREHBERICHT VOM FILM „DIE WEISSE HÖLLE VOM PIZ PALÜ".
Die Filmwoche, Nr. 44, 30. Oktober 1929.

Riefenstahl, Leni:
5 MONATE IN DER „HÖLLE".
Mein Film, Nr. 207, Wien 1929.

Ohne Autor:
FILMARBEIT WIE NOCH NIE – EIN GESPRÄCH MIT LENI RIEFENSTAHL
(über „Sieg des Glaubens"), Mein Film, Nr. 238, Wien 1932.

Riefenstahl, Leni:
WIE ICH SEPP RIST ENTDECKTE.
8 Uhr Blatt Nürnberg, 16. Juni 1933.

Alice:
JUNG SEIN UND SCHÖN BLEIBEN.
Plaudereien mit Filmkünstlern: Leni Riefenstahl,
Filmwelt, Nr. 35, 27. August 1933.

Ohne Autor:
FILMKAMERAS AUF DEM REICHSPARTEITAG.
Eine Unterredung mit Leni Riefenstahl,
Völkischer Beobachter, Sondernummer 1934, 6.9.1934.

Riefenstahl, Leni:
„TRIUMPH DES WILLENS".
Wie wir den Reichsparteitag drehten,
Die Woche, 13. Oktober 1934.

Ohne Autor:
WIE DER REICHSPARTEITAGSFILM ENTSTEHT.
„Noch nie in der Welt hat sich ein Staat derart für einen
Film eingesetzt", Magdeburger Tageszeitung, 13. 1.1935.

von Wehenalp:
LENI RIEFENSTAHL ÜBER DEN REICHSPARTEITAGSFILM.
Der Angriff, 26. März 1935.

Riefenstahl, Leni:
WIE DER NEUE WEHRMACHTSFILM ENTSTAND.
Filmwoche, Nr. 52, 29. Dezember 1935.

Ohne Autor:
LENI RIEFENSTAHL ÜBER IHREN FILM
(über den Film „Triumph des Willens"), Film Journal, 14/1935.

Riefenstahl, Leni:
KRAFT UND SCHÖNHEIT DER JUGEND MÖGEN FILMISCHE FORM
GEFUNDEN HABEN.
Filmkurier, 31. Dezember 1937.

Riefenstahl, Leni:
SCHÖNHEIT UND KAMPF IN HERRLICHSTER HARMONIE.
Licht-Bild-Bühne, 13. April 1938.

Riefenstahl, Leni:
DER OLYMPIA-FILM.
Filmwoche, Nr. 16, 15. April 1938.

Ohne Autor:
GESPRÄCH MIT LENI RIEFENSTAHL.
So entstand „Das Blaue Licht",
Filmkurier, 24. September 1938.

Riefenstahl, Leni:
NOTIZEN ZU PENTHESILEA (1939).
Filmkritik XVI, 1. August 1972 S. 416–425

Riefenstahl, Leni:
ÜBER WESEN UND GESTALTUNG DES DOKUMENTARISCHEN FILMS.
Der deutsche Film, Zeitschrift für Filmkunst und
Filmwissenschaft, Berlin, Sonderausgabe, 1940/1941.

Ohne Autor:
„TIEFLAND" – ENDLICH AM START.
Ein Interview mit Leni Riefenstahl,
Aktuelle Film-Nachrichten, 5. Jg., Nr. 2, 20. Januar 1954.

Delahaye, Michel:
LENI ET LE LOUP.
Cahiers du Cinéma, n° 170, September 1965, pp. 42–63.
English edition:
INTERVIEW WITH LENI RIEFENSTAHL.
Sarris, Andrew: Interview with Film Directors, Avon,
New York 1967, pp. 386–402.

Riefenstahl, Leni:
ZÄRTLICH SIND DIE SCHWARZEN RIESEN.
Stern 51/1969, S. 84–98.

Flot, Y.:
BRÈVE RENCONTRE AVEC LENI RIEFENSTAHL (Interview),
Écran (Fr), 9 Novembre 1972, pp. 28–30.

Riefenstahl, Leni:
THE GAMES THAT SURVIVED.
Sunday Times Magazine, 1 October 1972.

Weigel, Herman:
INTERVIEW MIT LENI RIEFENSTAHL.
Filmkritik 8/1972.

Hitchen, Gordon:
LENI RIEFENSTAHL INTERVIEWED OCTOBER 11TH, 1971.
Film Culture (US), 56–57, Spring 1973, pp. 94–121.

Riefenstahl, Leni:
SO STILL WAR WEIHNACHTEN NOCH NIE.
Bunte 1/1975, S. 64–69.

Riefenstahl, Leni:
„NIE ANTISEMITIN GEWESEN".
Spiegel 11/1976.

Riefenstahl, Leni:
BERICHT ÜBER DAS „ABENTEUER KAU".
Foto Magazin 08/1976.

Riefenstahl, Leni:
LA VIE SECRÈTE DES NOUBA.
Photo n° 110, Novembre 1976, pp. 48–69.

Riefenstahl, Leni:
DIE NUBA VON KAU.
Bildbericht über den zweiten Aufenthalt der Fotografin
im Sudan. Europäische Bildungsgemeinschaft,
Stuttgart 1976.

Riefenstahl, Leni:
MEIN PARADIES AFRIKA.
in: Grzimek, B./Messner R./Riefenstahl, L./Tichy. H.:
Paradiese, Saphir, München 1978.
English edition:
MY PARADISE, AFRICA.
in: Grzimek, B./Messner R./Riefenstahl, L./Tichy. H.:
Visions of Paradise, Hodder & Stoughton,
London 1981.

Schreiber, Hermann:
IM GESPRÄCH MIT LENI RIEFENSTAHL.
in: Schreiber, Hermann: Lebensläufe. Hermann
Schreiber im Gespräch mit Joseph Beuys, Julius
Hackethal, Ernst Herhaus, Manfred Krug, Hans Küng,
Loriot, John Neumeier, Leni Riefenstahl, Ullstein
Verlag, Frankfurt am Main, Berlin, Wien 1980.

Riefenstahl, Leni:
BERICHT ÜBER DAS SCHAFFEN LENI RIEFENSTAHLS IN AFRIKA.
Westermanns Monatshefte, Oktober 1982.

Riefenstahl, Leni:
AFTER A HALF-CENTURY.
Leni Riefenstahl confronts the US army report that
exonerated her of War Crimes,
Film Culture (US), 79, Winter 1996, pp. 27–34.

Riefenstahl, Leni:
„MIR KAM NICHTS OBSKUR VOR"
Die Woche, 22. August 1997, S. 38.

Riefenstahl, Leni:
„REALITÄT HAT MICH NIE INTERESSIERT".
Über ihre Filme, ihr Schönheitsideal, ihre NS-Verstrickun-
gen und Hitlers Wirkung auf die Menschen,
Der Spiegel, Jg. 51, Heft 34/1997, S. 202–205.

Riefenstahl, Leni:
MEINE NUBA.
„Mein Photo des Jahrhunderts": Leni Riefenstahl über den
Stamm im Sudan, der ihr Leben veränderte,
Zeitmagazin, 23. April 1998.

Millot, Lorraine:
CROIX GOMMÉE. Leni Riefenstahl, 97 ans,
cinéaste allemande, Libération, 5 janvier 2000.

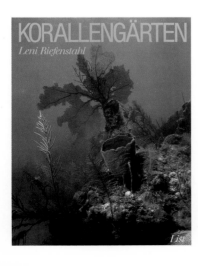
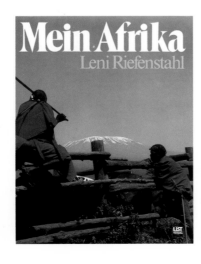

BÜCHER ÜBER LENI RIEFENSTAHL
BOOKS ON LENI RIEFENSTAHL

Kreimeier, Klaus:
FANCK – TRENKER – RIEFENSTAHL:
DER DEUTSCHE BERGFILM UND SEINE FOLGEN.
Stiftung Deutsche Kinemathek, Berlin 1972.

Barsam, Richard M.:
FILM GUIDE TO TRIUMPH OF THE WILL.
Series: Indiana University Press Film Guide Series, Indiana
University Press, Bloomington 1975.

Wallace, Peggy Ann:
A HISTORICAL STUDY OF THE CAREER OF LENI RIEFENSTAHL
FROM 1923 TO 1933.
Berkeley 1975.

Infield, Glenn B.:
LENI RIEFENSTAHL. THE FALLEN FILM GODDESS.
Thomas Y. Crowell, New York 1976.
Édition française:
LENI RIEFENSTAHL ET LE TROISIÈME REICH.
Traduit de l'americain par Véronique Chauveau, Seuil,
Paris 1978.
Japanese edition:
BETWEEN THE ART AND THE POLITICS.
Libro Port Press, Tokyo 1981.

Ford, Charles:
LENI RIEFENSTAHL.
Series: Filmmaker no. 29, La Table Ronde, Paris 1978.
Deutsche Ausgabe:
LENI RIEFENSTAHL – SCHAUSPIELERIN.
REGISSEURIN UND FOTOGRAFIN.
übersetzt von Antoinette Gittinger, Heyne, München 1982.

Hinton, David B.:
THE FILMS OF LENI RIEFENSTAHL.
The Scarecrow Press, Metuchen (NJ.), London 1978,
²1991, ³2000.

Berg-Pan, Renata:
LENI RIEFENSTAHL.
Twayne, Boston 1980.

Loiperdinger, Martin:
„TRIUMPH DES WILLENS" – EINSTELLUNGSPROTOKOLL
DES FILMS VON LENI RIEFENSTAHL.
Filmland-Presse, München 1980.

Graham, Cooper C.:
A HISTORICAL AND AESTHETIC ANALYSIS OF
LENI RIEFENSTAHL'S „OLYMPIA".
Ann Arbor University Microfilms International, Michigan
1984.

Quaresima, Leonardo:
LENI RIEFENSTAHL.
La Nuova Italia, Firenze 1984.

Culbert, David:
LENI RIEFENSTAHL'S TRIUMPH OF THE WILL.
Series: Research collections in the social history of commu-
nications, University Publications of America, Frederick,
MD 1986.

Graham, Cooper C.:
LENI RIEFENSTAHL AND OLYMPIA.
Based in part on the author's thesis – New York University,
Series: Filmmakers no. 13, The Scarecrow Press, Metuchen
(NJ.), London 1986.

Loiperdinger, Martin:
RITUALE DER MOBILMACHUNG – DER PARTEITAGSFILM „TRIUMPH DES
WILLENS" VON LENI RIEFENSTAHL.
Leske und Budrich, Opladen 1987.

Smith, David Calvert:
TRIUMPH OF THE WILL: A FILM BY LENI RIEFENSTAHL.
Original shooting script never before released, as written by
Leni Riefenstahl herself, scene by scene shot list (366 scenes), selected still picture reproductions of unpublished scenes from the film (80 pictures), translated from the original
shooting script in German, Series: Chronicle film script
series, Celluloid Chronicles Press, Richardson, Texas 1990.

Yamazaki, Yoko:
WOMEN WHO BECAME „THE LEGEND".
Kodan-sha press, Tokyo 1990 & 1994.

Aas, Nils Klevjer:
FASCISMENS FASCINASJON – ET DIDAKTISK DILEMMA:
LENI RIEFENSTAHLS „VILJENS TRIUMF" SOM KILDEMATERIALE OG
PÅVIRKNINGSKILDE.
Statens filmsentral, Oslo 1991.

Ishioka, Eiko:
LENI RIEFENSTAHL – LIFE.
Photographer Leni Riefenstahl, producer and art director
Eiko Ishioka, text in Japanese, Kyuryudo Art Pub. Co.,
Tokyo 1991.

Hoffmann, Hilmar:
MYTHOS OLYMPIA.
Autonomie und Unterwerfung von Sport und Kultur:
Hitlers Olympiade, olympische Kultur und Riefenstahls
Olympia-Film, Aufbau Verlag, Berlin 1993.

Vernet, Sandrine/Gerke, Klaus:
LENI RIEFENSTAHL: LE POUVOIR DES IMAGES.
Dossier réuni par Sandrine Vernet & Klaus Gerke, Forme
écrite d'une discussion avec Hilmar Hoffmann, Erwin Lei-
ser, Bernhard Eisenschitz, Hans-Peter Kochenrath, Frieda
Grafe, Francis Courtade sous la direction de Frédéric
Mitterrand, ZDF/Arte von 1993, K. films èd, Paris 1995.

Bignardi, Irene/Borghese, Alessandra/Falzone Del Barbarò:
LENI RIEFENSTAHL. IL RITMO DI UNO SGUARDO.
(Milano, Palazzo della Ragione; 10 luglio – 6 ottobre
1996), Leonardo Arte Milano, Milano 1996.
English version:
LENI RIEFENSTAHL.
Art Books International 1997.

Defeni, Sonie:
„DAS BLAUE LICHT"
La leggenda della regista Leni Riefenstahl, tese di laurea in
lingue e letterature straniere, Istituto Universitario di
Lingue Moderne, Facoltá di Lingue e Letterature Straniere,
Feltre 1996.

Salkeld, Audrey:
A PORTRAIT OF LENI RIEFENSTAHL.
Originally published: Jonathan Cape, London 1996.
New edition: Pimlico, London 1997.

Phillips, Peggy:
TWO WOMEN UNDER WATER: A CONFESSION.
Fithian Press, Santa Barbara 1998.

Filmmuseum Potsdam (Hg.):
LENI RIEFENSTAHL.
Mit Beiträgen von Oksana Bulgakowa, Bärbel Dalichow,
Claudia Lenssen, Felix Moeller, Georg Seeßlen, Ines Walk,
Henschel Verlag, Berlin 1999.

Camera Work (Hg.):
LENI RIEFENSTAHL.
Katalog zur Ausstellung vom 6. Mai bis 24. Juni 2000 in
der Galerie Camera Work in Berlin, mit einem Text von
Michael Krüger, Berlin 2000.

AUSGEWÄHLTE ARTIKEL UND AUFSÄTZE
ZU LENI RIEFENSTAHL
SELECTED ARTICLES AND ESSAYS
ON LENI RIEFENSTAHL

Allgeier, Sepp:
DIE JAGD NACH DEM BILD.
18 Jahre als Kameramann in Arktis und Hochgebirge.
Stuttgart: Engelhorn 1931.

Weiss, Trude:
THE BLUE LIGHT.
Close Up, 9 February 1932.

Ohne Autor:
BAHNBRECHENDER ERFOLG IN DEN VEREINIGTEN STAATEN.
Amerikanische Pressestimmen über „Das Blaue Licht",
Film-Kurier, 6. November 1934.

Ohne Autor:
BOTSCHAFTERIN DES DEUTSCHEN FILMS.
Bericht über Leni Riefenstahls Vorträge in England,
Film-Kurier, 2. März 1943.

Kracauer, Siegfried:
FROM CALIGARI TO HITLER. A PSYCHOLOGICAL
HISTORY OF GERMAN FILM.
Princeton University Press, Princeton 1947, ²1966; Dobson,
London 1974.
Edizione italiana:
CINEMA TEDESCO: DAL „GABINETTO DEL DOTT. CALIGARI"
A HITLER (1918–1933).
Traduzione di Giuliana Baracco e Carlo D'Oglio, A.
Mondadori, Milano 1954.
Deutsche Ausgabe:
VON CALIGARI ZU HITLER. EINE PSYCHOLOGISCHE GESCHICHTE DES
DEUTSCHEN FILMS.
Übersetzt von Ruth Baumgarten und Karsten Witte,
Deutsche Erstausgabe Rowohlt, Hamburg 1958,
Neuausgabe: Suhrkamp Verlag, Frankfurt am Main 1979,
²1984, ³1993.
Edition française:
DE CALIGARI À HITLER: UNE HISTOIRE PSYCHOLOGIQUE
DU CINÉMA ALLEMAND.
Traduit de l'anglais par Claude B. Lebenson, L'Âge
d'homme, Lausanne 1973; reprint: Flammarion, Paris
1987.
Edición española:
KRACAUER. SIEGFRIED: DE CALIGARI A HITLER:
UNA HISTÒRIA PSICOLÒGICA DEL CINE ALEMÁN.
Traducción de Héctor Grossi, Paidós Ibèrica, Barcelona
1985, ²1995.
Finnish edition:
CALIGARISTA HITLERIIN: SAKSALAISEN ELOKUVAN
PSYKOLOGINEN HISTORIA.
Valtion painatuskeskus, Helsinki 1987.

Gunston, David:
LENI RIEFENSTAHL.
Film Quarterly, 14 January 1960.

Ohne Autor:
LENI RIEFENSTAHLS FALSCHE TRÄNEN.
Die Urheberrechte der Parteitagsfilme – Streit um Leisers
„Mein Kampf",
Kölner Rundschau, 14. Januar 1961.

Kuhlbrodt, Dietrich:
LENI RIEFENSTAHL WIEDER OFFIZIELL.
– In Bremen verherrlicht – Auf der Berlinale begrüßt,
Die Zeit, 24. Juli 1964.

Gardner, Robert:
CAN THE WILL TRIUMPH?.
Film Comment, vol. 3, no. 1, Winter 1965.

Brownlow, Kevin:
LENI RIEFENSTAHL.
Film (London), 47, Winter 1966–67.

Richards, Jeffrey:
LENI RIEFENSTAHL: STYLE AND STRUCTURE.
Silent Picture 8, Autumn 1970, pp. 17–19.

Alpert, Hollis:
THE LIVELY GHOST OF LENI.
Saturday Review, 25 March 1972.

Kreimeier, Klaus:
ZUM RIEFENSTAHL-HEFT DER „FILMKRITIK".
epd Kirche und Film, 25. September 1972.

Linder, Herbert (Redaktion):
LENI RIEFENSTAHL.
in: Filmkritik XVI, 01. August 1972.
Darin enthalten:
Weigel, Herman:
INTERVIEW MIT LENI RIEFENSTAHL.
S. 395–410 und
Randbemerkungen zum Thema
S. 426–433

Cocteau, Jean:
FOUR LETTERS BY JEAN COCTEAU TO LENI RIEFENSTAHL.
Film Culture (US), 56–57, Spring 1973, pp. 90–93.

DOSSIER FILMOGRAPHY.
Film Culture (US), no. 56–57, Spring 1973, p. 94–226.

Fanck, Arnold:
ER FÜHRTE REGIE MIT GLETSCHERN, STÜRMEN UND LAWINEN.
Ein Filmpionier erzählt. Nymphenburger Verlags-
Handlung, München 1973, S. 151–310.

HENRY JAWORSKY INTERVIEWED BY GORDON HITCHENS, KIRK BOND,
AND JOHN HANHARDT.
Film Culture (US), 56, Spring 1973.

Vogel, Amos:
CAN WE NOW FORGET THE EVIL THAT SHE DID?
New York Times, 13 May 1973.

Barkhausen, Hans:
FOOTNOTE TO THE HISTORY OF RIEFENSTAHL'S OLYMPIA.
Film Quarterly, 21 January 1974, pp. 8–12.

Vogel, Amos:
FILM AS SUBVERSIVE ART.
George Weidenfeld and Nicolson Ltd,
London 1974, ²1997.
Nederlandse uitgave:
DE FILM ALS TABOE-BREKER.
Übersetzer: A. Haakman, Gaade, Den Haag 1974.
Édition française:
LE CINÉMA: ART SUBVERSIF.
Traduit de l'américain par Claude Frégnac,
Éditions Buchet/Chastel, Paris 1977.
Deutsche Ausgabe:
FILM ALS SUBVERSIVE KUNST. KINO WIDER DIE TABUS – VON
EISENSTEIN BIS KUBRICK.
Aus dem Englischen übersetzt von Felix Bucher, Monika
Curths, Alexander Horwarth, Pierre Lachat und Gertrud
Strub, Robert Azderball, Hannibal Verlag, St. Andrä-
Wördern 1997, S. 173–180,

Sontag, Susan:
FASCINATING FASCISM.
New York Review of Books, 2 February 1975; reprint in:
Sontag, Susan: Under the Sign of Saturn, originally pub-
lished: Farrar, Straus & Giroux, New York 1980.
Reprint: Anchor Books, New York 1991; Writers and
readers, London 1980, ²1983;
Deutsche Ausgabe:
FASZINIERENDER FASCHISMUS.
Die Zeit, 02./09.03.1975; Der Artikel erschien auch in:
Frauen und Film, Heft 14, Rotbuch Verlag, Berlin 1977,
S. 6–18 und in Sontag, Susan: Im Zeichen des Saturn. Essays,
Carl Hanser Verlag, München 1981; Weitere Ausgabe im
Fischer Taschenbuch Verlag, Frankfurt/Main ²1990, S. 96–125.
Svensk upplagan:
I SATURNUS TECKEN.
Översättning. Eva Liljegren, Bromberg, Stockholm,
Uppsala 1981.
Edizione italiana:
SOTTO IL SEGNO DI SATURNO.
Traduzione di Stefania Bertola, Einaudi, Torino 1982.
Nederlandse uitgave:
IN HET TEKEN VAN SATURNUS.
Villa, Weesp 1984.
Édition française:
SOUS LE SIGNE DE SATURNE.
Traduit par Phillippe Blanchard [et al.], Seuil, Paris 1985.
Edición española:
BAJO EL SIGNO DE SATURNO.
Traducciòn de Juan Utrilla Trejo, Edhasa, Barcelona 1987.
Ukrainian edition:
MAGIČESKIJ FAŠIZM.
Iskusstvo Kino (UR), 6 June 1991, pp. 50–57.

Holthausen, Hans Egon:
LENI RIEFENSTAHL IN AMERIKA.
Zum Problem einer faschistischen Ästhetik,
Merkur 29 (1975), S. 569–578.

Jagger, Bianca:
LENI'S BACK AND BIANCA'S GOT HER.
Andy Warhol's Interview no. 5, January 1975

Steinert, Jörg:
DAS FEST DER MESSER UND DER LIEBE.
Stern Nr. 41, 2. Oktober 1975, S. 34–58.

Bittorf, Wilhelm:
BLUT UND HODEN.
Spiegel, Nr. 44/1976.

Sokal, Harry:
ÜBER NACHT ANTISEMITIN GEWORDEN?.
Spiegel, Nr. 46/1976.

Ohne Autor:
LENI RIEFENSTAHL UNTER DEN NUBA.
Bunte 37/1976, S. 44–53.

Hansen, Sven:
VON NÜRNBERG ZU DEN NUBA.
Die Welt, Ausgabe B, 20. August 1977.

Schille, Peter:
LENIS BLÜHENDE TRÄUME.
Stern, Nr. 35, 18. August 1977.

Schille, Peter:
ABSCHIED VON DEN NUBA.
Geo 9/1977 S. 6–32.

Ohne Autor:
MEIN WILDES LEBEN.
Quick 35/1977, S. 41–52.

Harmssen, Henning:
DER FALL LENI RIEFENSTAHL.
Neue Züricher Zeitung, 12. Januar 1978.

Rich, B. Ruby:
LENI RIEFENSTAHL: THE DECEPTIVE MYTH.
in: Erens, Patricia (Ed.), Sexual Stratagems: The World
of Women in Film, Horizon, New York 1979,
pp. 202–209.

von Wysocki, Gisela:
DIE BERGE UND DIE PATRIACHEN. LENI RIEFENSTAHL.
in: von Wysocki, Gisela: Die Fröste der Freiheit.
Aufbruchsphanatasien, Syndikat, Frankfurt/Main 1980.

Bergmann, Lutz:
DIE LENI MIT DER LEICA.
Bunte 34/1982, S. 20–24.

Grafe, Frieda:
RIEFENSTAHL.
in: Grafe, Frieda: Beschriebener Film. 1974–1985. Murnau,
Lubitsch, Renoir, Riefenstahl, Ophuels, Mizoguchi, Verlag
Die Republik, Salzhusen-Luhmuehlen 1985.

Leiser, Erwin:
VOM KONZENTRATIONSLAGER ZUM FILM – UND ZURÜCK.
Leni Riefenstahl wehrt sich gegen den Vorwurf, KZ-
Gefangene als Statisten zwangsverpflichtet zu haben,
Die Weltwoche, Nr. 10/7. März 1985.

Augstein, Rudolf:
LENI, DIE „FÜHRERBRAUT".
Der Spiegel, 33/1987, S. 75.

Doane, Mary Ann:
THE MOVING IMAGE: PHOTOS AND THE MATERNAL.
in: Doane, Mary Ann: The Desire to Desire. The Woman's
Film of the 1940s, Bloomington & Indianapolis 1987,
pp. 70–97.

Drews, Jürgen:
LENI RIEFENSTAHL. MIT 85 ENTDECKT SIE DIE SCHÖNHEIT DER TIEFE.
Bunte 48/1987, S. 88–102.

Mitscherlich, Maragarete:
TRIUMPH DER VERDRÄNGUNG.
Über die Filmregisseurin Leni Riefenstahl und die
Memorien der glühenden Hitler-Verehrerin,
Stern 49/1987.

Spiess-Hohnholz, M.:
VERLORENER KAMPF UM DIE ERINNERUNG.
Der Spiegel, Nr. 33/1987.

Loiperdinger, Martin/Culbert, David:
LENI RIEFENSTAHL, THE SA, AND THE NAZI PARTY RALLY FILMS,
NURENBERG 1933–34: SIEG DES GLAUBENS UND TRIUMPH DES
WILLENS.
Historical Journal of Film, Radio and Television (UK),
VIII/1, 1988, pp. 3–38.

Loiperdinger, Martin:
HALB DOKUMENT, HALB FÄLSCHUNG.
Zur Inszenierung der Eröffnungsfeier in Leni Riefenstahls
Olympia-Film „Fest der Völker",
Medium, 1988, 18. Jahrgang., Heft 3, S. 42–62.

Rentschler, Eric:
FATAL ATTRACTIONS: LENI RIEFENSTAHL'S „THE BLUE LIGHT".
October no. 48, Spring 1989, pp. 46–68.

Rentschler, Eric:
MOUNTAINS AND MODERNITY: RELOCATING THE BERGFILM.
New German Critique 51 (1990), pp. 137–161.

Sander-Brahms, Helma:
TIEFLAND: TYRANNENMORD.
In: Prinzler, Hans Helmut (Hg.): Das Jahr 1945: Filme aus
15 Ländern, ein Katalog zur Retrospektive der 40.
Internationalen Filmfestspiele Berlin 1990, Stiftung
Deutsche Kinemathek, Berlin 1990, S. 173–176.

Reichelt, Peter:
„VOLKSGEMEINSCHAFT" UND FÜHRERKULT/„FEST DER SCHÖNHEIT" UND
SPIELE DER GEWALT: OLYMPIA 1936.
in: Reichelt, Peter: Der schöne Schein des Dritten Reiches –
Faszination und Gewalt des Faschismus, München 1991,
S. 114–138, S. 162–172.

Vetten, Detlef:
SCHÖNE WELT AM RIFF.
Stern 19/1991, S. 62–74.

Culbert, David/Loiperdinger, Martin:
LENI RIEFENSTAHL'S TAG DER FREIHEIT: THE NAZI PARTY RALLY FILM.
Historical Journal of Film, Radio and Television, 1992,
vol. 12, no. 1, pp. 3–40.

Elsaesser, Thomas:
LENI RIEFENSTAHL: THE BODY BEAUTIFUL. ART CINEMA AND FASCIST
AESTHETICS.
in: Cook, Pam/Dodd, Phillip (Ed.), Women in Film: A Sight
and Sound Reader, Temple UP, Philadelphia 1992,
pp. 186–197.

Knef, Hildegard:
NICHTS ALS NEUGIER.
Interviews zu Fragen der Parapsychologie mit Gabriele
Hoffmann, Kardinal König, Professor Pritz, Bruno Kreisky,
Niki Lauda, Reinhold Messner, Henry Miller, Lilli Palmer,
Leni Riefenstahl, Carrol Righter, Françoise Sagan,
Gütersloh, o.J.

Kreimeier, Klaus:
DIE UFA-STORY.
Geschichte eines Filmkonzerns, Carl Hanser Verlag,
München, Wien 1992, S. 271–273, 296–299.
English edition:
THE UFA-STORY:
A history of Germany's greatest film company, 1918–1945,
translated by Robert and Rita Kimber, Hill & Wang, New
York 1996.
Édition française:
UNE HISTOIRE DU CINÉMA ALLEMAND, LA UFA.
Traduit par l'allemand par Olivier Mannoni, Flammarion,
Paris 1994.

Quaresima, Leonardo:
ARNOLD FANCK – AVANTGARDIST: „DER HEILIGE
BERG"/KINEMATOGRAPHIE ALS RITUELLE ERFAHRUNG.
in: Bock, Hans Michael/Töteberg, Michael in Zusammen-
arbeit mit Cine-Graph – Hamburgisches Zentrum für
Filmforschung e.V. (Hg.): Das Ufa-Buch: die internationale
Geschichte von Deutschlands größtem Film-Konzern;
Kunst und Krisen, Stars und Regisseure, Wirtschaft und
Politik, Verlag Zweitausendundeins, Frankfurt/Main,
S. 250–252, S. 372–374.

Schiff, Stephan:
LENI'S OLYMPIA.
Why did Leni Riefenstahl, publishing her memoirs this
month in the U.K., choose to become the documentarian
of the Third Reich?, Vanity Fair, 1 September 1992 vol. 55,
no. 9, pp. 251–296.

Seeßlen, Georg:
DAS MÄDCHEN, DAS KRIEGER SEIN WOLLTE.

– Zu Leni Riefenstahls Filmen und Bildern –
aus Anlaß des 90. Geburtstages,
Der Tagesspiegel, 22. August 1992.

Cauby, Vincent:
LENI RIEFENSTAHL IN A LONG CLOSE-UP.
New York Times, 14 October 1993.

Corliss, Richard:
RIEFENSTAHL'S LAST TRIUMPH.
Time, 18 October 1993, pp. 91–92.

Culbert, David:
LENI RIEFENSTAHL AND THE DIARIES OF JOSEPH GOEBBELS.
Historical Journal of Film, Radio and Television (UK), 13,
1 March 1993, pp. 85–93.

Faris, J. C.:
LENI RIEFENSTAHL AND THE NUBA PEOPLE OF KORDOFAN PROVINCE.
Historical Journal of Film, Radio and Television (UK), 13,
1 March 1993, pp. 95–97.

Foss, Kim:
DET TREDJE RIGES FALDUE ENGEL.
Kosmorama (Denmark), XXXIX/203, Spring 1993,
pp. 40–44.

Hoffmann, Hilmar:
EINFÜHRUNG ZU OLYMPIA. MENETEKEL DER VERGANGENHEIT
FÜR DIE ZUKUNFT – NACHBETRACHTUNGEN ZU LENI RIEFENSTAHLS
OLYMPIAFILM/SPORT UND RASSE.
in: Cine Marketing GmbH (Hg.): Sport und Film: bewegte
Körper – bewegte Bilder, Internationale Sportfilmtage
Berlin 1993, Redaktion: Anette C. Eckert, Thomas Til
Redevagen, Aufbau Verlag, Berlin 1993, S. 98–101,
S. 108–113.

Niroumand, Miriam:
BILDER AN DIE MACHT.
tageszeitung, 30. Dezember 1993.

Panitz, Hans Jürgen:
FANCK. TRENKER. RIEFENSTAHL.
in: Berg '93 (Alpenvereinsjahrbuch), München – Innsbruck
– Bozen 1993.

Schlüpmann, Heide:
TRUGBILDER WEIBLICHER AUTONOMIE IM NATIONAL-
SOZIALISTISCHEN FILM. LENI RIEFENSTAHLS OLYMPIA:
TRIUMPH DES WEIBLICHEN WILLENS?
in: Cine Marketing GmbH (Hg.): Sport und Film: bewegte
Körper – bewegte Bilder, Internationale Sportfilmtage
Berlin 1993, Redaktion: Anette C. Eckert, Thomas Til
Redevagen, Aufbau Verlag, Berlin 1993, S. 102–107.

Simon, John:
THE FÜHRER'S MOVIE MAKER.
New York Times Book Review, 26 September 1993,
pp. 1, 26–29.

Witte, Karsten:
FILM IM NATIONALSOZIALISMUS.
in: Jacobsen, Kaes, Prinzler (Hg.): Geschichte des deutschen
Films, Stuttgart 1993, S. 124–133.

Compare, Manohla Dargis:
QUEEN OF DENIAL:
The life and lies of Leni Riefenstahl,
Voice Literary Supplement 123, March 1994.

Elsaesser, Thomas:
PORTRAIT OF THE ARTIST AS A YOUNG WOMAN.
Sight and Sound (London), 1994, vol. 3, no. 2, pp. 15–18.

Hausschild, Joachim/Sibylle Bergmann:
EINE FRAU MIT VERGANGENHEIT.
Stern TV, März 1994, S. 4–9.

Holthof, Marc:
DE WITTE EXTASE:
Over Berlusconi, bergfilms en de geest van München,
Andere Sinema (Belgium), no. 121, May-June 1994,
p. 17–21.

Mitscherlich, Margarete:
EINE DEUTSCHE FRAU – LENI RIEFENSTAHL.
in: Mitscherlich, Margarete: Über die Mühsal der
Emanzipation, Frankfurt/Main 1994.

Mulder, Arjen:
DEN KONNTE ICH NICHT OPTISCH ZEIGEN.
Andere Sinema (Belgium), no. 121, May-June 1994, pp. 13–16.

Schlapper, Martin:
EIN MONUMENT DER EINSICHTSLOSIGKEIT.
„Die Macht der Bilder – Leni Riefenstahl",
Neue Züricher Zeitung, 26. November 1994.

Seeßlen, Georg:
DIE MACHT DER BILDER.
epd Film, 4/1994.

Sklar, Robert:
THE DEVIL'S DIRECTOR. HER TALENT WAS HER TRAGEDY.
Cineaste (US), XX/3, 1994, pp. 18–23.

Sudendorf, Werner:
NICHT ZUR VERÖFFENTLICHUNG.
Zur Biografie des Filmjournalisten Ernst (Ejott) Jäger,
In: Filmexil (Stiftung Deutsche Kinemathek Berlin),
Heft 5, Dezember 1994, S. 61–66.

Weidinger, Brigitte:
DIE MACHT DER BILDER
– WIE DIE ARD AUF RAY MÜLLERS FILM REAGIERTE.
Süddeutsche Zeitung, 9./10. April 1994.

Ohne Autor:
KEINE HOMMAGE AN LENI RIEFENSTAHL.
– Interview mit Regisseur Ray Müller, Frankfurter
Allgemeine Zeitung, 26. März 1994.

Duerr, Hans Peter:
DAS BEISPIEL DER ALTEN GRIECHEN UND DER NUBA.
in: Duerr, Hans Peter: Frühstück im Grünen. Essays und
Interviews, Suhrkamp Verlag, Frankfurt am Main 1995,
S. 52–77.

Neubauer, Ruodlieb:
92 JAHRE – UND KEINE SCHEU VOR NEUER TECHNIK. LENI RIEFENSTAHL
ZU IHREM NEUEN FILM.
Professional Production, Nr. 90, Juli/August 1995, S. 12–14.

Veld, Renee in't:
RIEFENSTAHL.
in: Veld, Renée in't: Uit liefde voor de Fuehrer vrouwen van
het Derde Rijk: Eva Braun, Magda Goebbels, Leni
Riefenstahl, Florrie Rost van Tonningen, Winifred Wagner,
Walburg Pers, Zutphen 1995.

von Dassanowsky, Robert:
„WHEREVER YOU MAY RUN. YOU CANNOT ESCAPE HIM":
Leni Riefenstahl's self-reflection and romantic
transcendence of Nazism in Tiefland,
Camera Obscura (US), no. 35, May 1995, pp. 106–129.

Lenssen, Claudia:
DIE FÜNF KARRIEREN DER LENI RIEFENSTAHL.
epd-film, 1/1996.

Manzoli, G.:
LA BELLA MALEDETTA.
Cineforum, XXXVI/358, October 1996, p. 38–45.

Müller, Almut/Pottmeier, Gregor:
FASCHISMUS UND AVANTGARDE.
– Leni Riefenstahls „Triumph des Willens", in: Müller,
Almut/Pottmeier, Gregor: Das kalte Bild – Neue Studien
zum NS-Propagandafilm, Augen-Blick, Marburger
Hefte zur Medienwissenschaft, Nr. 22, Januar 1996,
S. 39–58.

Rentschler, Eric:
A LEGEND FOR MODERN TIME: THE BLUE LIGHT.
in: Rentschler, Eric: Ministry of Illusion. Nazi Cinema and
its Afterlife, Harvard University Press, Cambridge, London
1996, pp. 27–52.

Soussloff, Catherine/Nichols, Bill:
LENI RIEFENSTAHL:
The Power of the Image, Discource, Spring 1996, vol. 18,
no. 3, p. 20.

Nowinska, Ewa:
LENI RIEFENSTAHL: DIE REGISSEURIN VON MACHT UND SCHÖNHEIT.
in: Olivier, Antje/Braun, Sevgi: Anpassung oder Verbot:
Künstlerinnen und die 30er Jahre – Vicki Baum, Eta

Harich-Schneider, Clara Haskil, Hannah Höch, Else
Lasker-Schüler, Lotte Lenya, Erika Mann, Leni Riefenstahl,
Charlotte Salomon, Mary Wigman/Gret Palucca, Droste
Verlag, Düsseldorf 1997, S. 263–294.

Rapp, Christian:
HÖHENRAUSCH: DER DEUTSCHE BERGFILM.
Sonderzahl Verlagsgesellschaft m.b.H., Wien 1997,
S. 105–156.

Yoshida, Kazuhiko:
MEDIA AND FASCISM (1)
An Inquiry about Leni Riefenstahl, Hosei Riron, 1 No-
vember 1997, vol. 30, no. 2, p. 202, text in Japanese.

Sigmund, Anna Maria:
LENI RIEFENSTAHL: DIE AMAZONENKÖNIGIN.
in: Sigmund, Anna: Die Frauen der Nazis, Wien 1998,
S. 99–117.

Hake, Sabine:
OF SEEING AND OTHERNESS: LENI RIEFENSTAHL'S AFRICAN
PHOTOGRAPHS.
in: Friedrichmeyer, Sara/Kennox, Sara/Zantop, Susanne:
The imperialist imagination, Series: Social history, popular
culture, and politics in Germany, Ann Arbor: University of
Michigan Press 1999.

Schühly, Thomas:
LENI RIEFENSTAHL – DIE MACHT DER BILDER.
Welt am Sonntag, Nr. 21, 23. Mai 1999, S. 44.

Schwarzer, Alice:
LENI RIEFENSTAHL. PROPAGANDISTIN ODER KÜNSTLERIN.
EMMA, Januar/Februar 1999.

Werneburg, Brigitte:
RIEFENSTAHL'S RETURN.
Art of America, October 1999

Müller, Ray:
DER BESUCH DER ALTEN DAME.
Stern 14/2000, S. 63–70.

INTERNET BIBLIOGRAFIE
INTERNET BIBLIOGRAPHY

The Perpetual Dancer. Celebrating the Art of Leni
Riefenstahl. Extract from the catalog on a current UK
exhibition on the work of Leni Riefenstahl (2000):
http://www.leniriefenstahl.co.uk/

Internet Resources on Leni Riefenstahl:
http://www.webster.edu/~barrettb/riefenstahl2.htm

Flippo, Hyde: Leni Riefenstahl. Links, films and books
(1998–2000):
http://www.german-way.com/cinema/rief2.html

von Dassanowsky, Robert: „Wherever you may run, you
cannot escape him". Leni Riefenstahl's self-reflection and
romantic transcendence of Nazism in Tiefland (originally
published in Camera Obscura no. 35, May 1995):
www.powernet.net/~hflippo/cinema/tiefland.html

Ausschnitte aus den Filmen von Leni Riefenstahl sind in
dem preisgekrönten dreistündigen Dokumentarfilm
LENI RIEFENSTAHL – DIE MACHT DER BILDER (1993) von Ray Müller
zu sehen, einer englisch-deutsch-belgischen Co-Produktion.

Excerpts from Leni Riefenstahl's films can be seen in Ray
Müller's three-hour documentary THE WONDERFUL. HORRIBLE
LIFE OF LENI RIEFENSTAHL (1993), an English-German-Belgian
coproduction, which has received various international
awards.

Des extraits de films de Leni Riefenstahl figurent dans
le documentaire de trois heures LE POUVOIR DES IMAGES –
LENI RIEFENSTAHL (1993) de Ray Müller, une coproduction
anglaise, allemande et belge, récompensée au niveau
international.